We can all successfully grow our businesses — on any economy. Here's how!

Pat

Praise for *Defy Gravity*

"*Defy Gravity* is an insightful book. Its metaphor of flight creates images that are memorable and actionable. Rebel's approach will help you recognize what's holding you back—empowering you to reach for and attain your business objectives."
—Ed Glassmeyer, managing partner, Oak Investment Partners

"If you run a company—or want to run one—*Defy Gravity* offers fascinating insights into defining your market, quantifying your value, and creating high-velocity sales growth."
—Randy Gage, author of *Prosperity Mind*

"Want to sustainably and profitably grow your business? *Defy Gravity* is for you. Rebel gives you the tools you need in her action-oriented book, chock-full of proven strategies, real-world examples and commonsense approaches. Read this book and make your business fly."
—Ed Niehaus, Collaborative Drug Discovery

"As a pilot and CEO, *Defy Gravity*'s principles of business flight resonated with me. This book offers powerful insight into business cultures, market dynamics and revolutionary ways to think about, and achieve, profitable growth. *Defy Gravity* is all you need to reach escape velocity and leave your competition in the rearview mirror forever!"
—Casey Powell, former CEO, Sequent Computer Systems; general manager of Microprocessor Operations, Intel

"In a world where good enough isn't good enough anymore, Rebel Brown has pulled together the right strategies, tips and thought-provoking advice to help your company soar. If you and your team are ready to defy gravity—this book will get you started."
—Joan Koerber-Walker, corporate executive, entrepreneur, and investor

"*Defy Gravity* is one of the most valuable business books for 2010 and beyond."
—Joe Levy, president and CEO, The Quadragon Group

"Most strategy books focus on concept and leave the reader to figure out the 'how to.' *Defy Gravity* delivers powerful yet practical strategic thinking, along with tactical recommendations, proven in real-world business. It's the answer we've all been looking for."
—Rob Butler, president, PayFlex Systems

"*Defy Gravity* takes business strategy to a whole new level. Rebel offers innovative yet proven approaches to power breakout business growth."
—Mike Fields, chairman, KANA Software

"Rebel Brown's provocative and easily understood ideas will inspire twenty-first century business leaders to lead and grow their firms in bold new ways. It's a must read for executives intent on making sure their companies are first movers in the increasingly competitive global economy."
—Gary J. Beach, publisher emeritus, *CIO* magazine

"*Defy Gravity* is a must read to compete in today's fast-moving market. It surely is a one-of-a-kind business book. To grow your business, read this book."
—Rick Thau, founder, CEO, and managing director, Thaughtful Transitions

"*Defy Gravity* is one of those books whose time has come. Change is not hard. Change is the only reality there is and the sooner organizations embrace it as the source of all opportunity the better. Is there a source of opportunity other than change or urgent need for it? I don't know of one."
—Ralph Talmont, CEO, Pixengo

"I can fly! And so can you, thanks to this great book from Rebel Brown. You'll loose the surly bonds of your business gravity and discover how your Value Mix will have you soaring to the heights of profit and competitive advantage."
—Wally Bock, business writer, coach, and consultant

"Rebel is the real deal and *Defy Gravity* is the best strategy book I've seen in years. From critical business concepts to applications in the real world to questions and exercises for all of us—*Defy Gravity* gives us all the tools we need to power profitability."
—Doug Michels, cofounder and CEO, The Santa Cruz Operation (SCO) and Tarantella

"One-dimensional thinking doesn't work anymore. *Defy Gravity* picks up where *The Innovator's Dilemma* left off; helping us navigate in four dimensions with new instincts and new rules. A must read for any modern business executive."
—Dave Bernstein, vice president and general manager of cloud computing, Cisco Systems

"Move over, status quo; there's a big new dynamic world out there. *Defy Gravity* will unleash your company's potential for success."
—Michael Welts, serial entrepreneur and marketing strategist

"Rebel does it again! A very informative, hold-no-punches book that gets to the roots of business dilemmas and suggests solutions. A must for growth-type companies."
—Tsvi Gal, general partner, Exigen Capital; former CTO, Deutsche Bank's Investment Bank and Asset Management

"Rebel Brown has achieved a soaring success with *Defy Gravity*. Whether you are a small business owner or a corporate titan, there is gold in the case studies shared, the wisdom applied, and the high-flying metaphors of business compared to a flight plan. *Defy Gravity* is clearly the fast path to take your business from grounded or crashing to a smooth ride and profit-filled future."
—Melissa Galt, chief prosperity officer, Prosper By Design

"*Defy Gravity*'s principles of business flight are a must read and follow for any businessperson. Whether you're an entrepreneur or a chief executive officer—read this book and ditch your gravity. Those who do will lead tomorrow—those who don't, well, they run out of runway."
—Bob Pette, vice president of the Professional Solutions Group, NVIDIA

"To go where we want to go, we have to break with status quo. Fortunately, Rebel Brown brings defying gravity down to earth with words, structure, logic and especially stories, showing us how to do it. *Defy Gravity* is an ideal gift to lift entrepreneurs to grow."
—Trey Pennington, social media expert, author of *Spitball Marketing*

"Rebel Brown's *Defy Gravity* provides dynamic and time-tested wisdom that will clearly delineate successful strategies for business growth. If you want to propel your company to new heights, then I highly recommend that you read and learn from *Defy Gravity*."
—Gil Namur, president, Synaptic Systems; president and CEO, Life As A Human

"It's a brave new world in business, and the old rules don't work anymore. *Defy Gravity* is exactly what businesses large and small need to profitably prosper—fast. This book is a must read for any business leader seeking sustainable growth. Run, don't walk, and get your copy today!"
—Stephanie Frank, bestselling author of *The Accidental Millionaire*

"*Defy Gravity* is filled with fresh strategies to escape the pull of the status quo, capture emerging opportunities and achieve high-velocity growth."
—Jill Konrath, bestselling author of *SNAP Selling* and *Selling to Big Companies*

DEFY GRAVITY

Propel Your Business *to* High-Velocity Growth

REBEL BROWN

GREENLEAF
BOOK GROUP PRESS

Published by Greenleaf Book Group Press
Austin, Texas
www.gbgpress.com

Distributed by Greenleaf Book Group LLC

For ordering information or special discounts for bulk purchases, please contact Greenleaf Book Group LLC at PO Box 91869, Austin, TX 78709, 512.891.6100.

Design and composition by Greenleaf Book Group LLC and Alex Head
Cover design by Greenleaf Book Group LLC
Cover photo by Sherry Lingle, Liquid Steel Photography

Publisher's Cataloging-In-Publication Data
(Prepared by The Donohue Group, Inc.)

Brown, Rebel.
   Defy gravity : propel your business to high-velocity growth / Rebel Brown. -- 1st ed.
   p. ; cm.
   "Defy gravity" is printed upside down on both cover and title pages.
   ISBN: 978-1-60832-054-7

   1. Strategic planning. 2. Business planning. 3. Corporations--Growth. 4. Organizational change. 5. Success in business. I. Title. II. Title: Propel your business to high-velocity growth
HD30.28   .B76 2010
658.4   2010927741

Part of the Tree Neutral™ program, which offsets the number of trees consumed in the production and printing of this book by taking proactive steps, such as planting trees in direct proportion to the number of trees used: www.treeneutral.com

TreeNeutral

Printed in the United States of America on acid-free paper

10 11 12 13 14   10 9 8 7 6 5 4 3 2

First Edition

For my Mom.

You always said I was born to be a writer.

Here I am, Mom. Thanks to you . . .

CONTENTS

We either climb higher or we crash and burn. The status quo doesn't cut it anymore.

Releasing the status quo is our first step toward sustainable growth.

Even as we lift them higher, our best sellers may be dragging us down.

Revenue is not the best measurement of a great customer.

But is it an opportunity for big success or big failure?

What happens when we outgrow our key employees?

Following our competitors will not make us market leaders.

Don't bet your business on those numbers.

Big Bang changes wreak havoc on our ability to grow.

Winning value is not created by volume; it's created by focus.

Value is in the eye of the beholder.

When Rebel Brown advises executives, business owners, and managers about getting back on track, expanding into new markets, or avoiding financial disaster, they owe it to their stakeholders and employees to sit up, listen well, and heed her words. When she writes an entire book on the subject, it's the chance of a lifetime, and all of us would do well to sit down, read closely, and follow her advice.

The message of *Defy Gravity* is simple enough: how to achieve sustainable growth in today's volatile and precarious marketplace. You might think of this book as Business 101, with its good, solid counsel enhanced and made clearer with concrete examples, thoughtful exercises, and illustrations. But it's really Advanced Placement Strategy. It offers a superior level of knowledge built from Brown's firsthand experiences in strategically positioning and launching more than 100 companies in her twenty years as a corporate coach and combined with her willingness to turn everything we think we know and trust on its ear.

Quite expertly, the author zooms in on what is important. She explains how businesses can "defy gravity" by avoiding the common mistakes that drag them down. She offers reasons why companies remain grounded, fall from the sky, or are forced to make emergency landings. She tells us how to become "dynamic," which is a key element in lifting our businesses toward profitable growth. She surprises us with key insights, such as the fact that a company's real competition is the status quo. She talks at length about value—company value, product value, and market value—and explains why value is like the fuel that keeps an airplane flying. Finally, Rebel Brown helps us map out a detailed flight plan that allows us to truly see that, when we think differently and question our logic born of the status quo, the sky's the limit for our growth. She leaves us empowered, knowing that we, too, can soar into the stratosphere of business profitability. It's all about focusing forward and constantly adjusting to match the dynamic winds of our markets.

I know Rebel Brown. We're in the same business, and there are very few people I respect as much as I do her. Her business acumen is right on target. It's the reason so many companies across the globe have tasted, and still feast upon, success. Truth is, after I finished reading a draft of this book, my first thought was that I wished I had written it. Simply put, it's brilliant. And now, more than ever, it is a book that is needed. The smallest businesses and the largest enterprises alike will benefit greatly from reading, studying, and applying *Defy Gravity*.

Thank you, Rebel, for releasing your brilliance! You are the pilot and we are your passengers flying toward business growth. Fly, Rebel, fly!

—Simon T. Bailey
Author of *Release Your Brilliance*

ACKNOWLEDGMENTS

First, I want to thank all of my clients throughout the years. Our experiences, and the trust you placed in me, formed the foundation of *Defy Gravity*. This book wouldn't exist without each and every one of you.

A heartfelt thanks to the fabulous partners at Oak Investment Partners for their long-term and continued support of my consulting business. Ed, Fred, David, Ifty and Ren—you all believed in me, and my abilities, even in the tough accounts. Thanks for all the opportunities!

To my business partner and sister-who-God-forgot-to-give me, Ardath Albee—where would I be without you? I'm here today, thanks to your insistence that I was, indeed, ready to live my dream and write my books. You were right and I won't look back!

To my fabulous publisher, Greenleaf Book Group—you rock! I had a dream of how my publisher would be—and after some pretty big nightmares with others, you made my dream come true! Clint Greenleaf—your team went above and beyond in every way! Justin Branch, Matt Donnelley, Carrie Winsett, Kristen Sears—you kept me sane and on track, well . . . most of the time. Alex Head, Neil Gonzalez and Sheila Parr—you captured just the designs I wanted to bring the concepts behind *Defy Gravity* to life. Linda O'Doughda, thanks for all the times you preceded your questions with "mi scuzi" to get me to sharpen my prose and for your excellent copyediting. Last but never least—Lari Bishop—you are a rock star! *Defy Gravity* is as much a result of my expertise as it is your knowledgeable and patient editorial guidance.

To my shepherd and marketing guru, Thom Scott—you are a force to behold! Thanks for teaching me the ropes of the author and speaker world. I am where I am today because of your patient and gracious support. And we've only just begun!

To Simon T. Bailey, my Brilliant Master—your support has been the light that keeps me shining even on the dull days. Thanks for lighting my path.

To Scott McKain, my friend and mentor—you stepped up and supported me from the beginning, even before *Defy Gravity* had soared onto the pages. Thanks for the introductions, the guidance and most of all for your friendship!

To David Brock and Mark Schaefer—thanks for the invaluable inputs in the early drafts, the ongoing discussions and your friendship!

To Doug Phillips and Bob Davis—thanks for being the men who support my financial and home world so I can focus on the business of Rebel. Having you in my corner makes it so much easier to live the life of my dreams!

Shawn, Katherine, Heather, Linda, Leslie, Kim, Deb, MB and all my friends who supported me through the book and so much more—thanks for believing in me, and my ability to soar!

And finally, thanks to Mike Fields. You helped me start my consulting business some twenty years ago. You believed in me and pushed me to soar. Thanks to you, I can and do Defy Gravity!

Principles of
Business Flight

Status quo doesn't cut it anymore.
We either climb higher or we crash and burn.

I almost crashed and burned off the coast of northern California. My parasail was blown back by a wind gust. I blew back before I knew what hit me—straight toward power lines and a very busy freeway. I collapsed my paragliding wing and fell thirty feet to the ground to avoid an even worse outcome. Not fun, but I learned a lot that day.

It was my first flight on a brand-new paragliding wing: quicker and more responsive to the wind—a Corvette compared to my older town car. I assumed that this wing would respond pretty much the same way as my older one did.

Our past doesn't always apply to our present.

I was focused on a hawk when the gust hit me. She'd been following me for awhile. Hawks often fly with parasailers. I love to watch them lift and float by simply changing their wing feathers, as I work so hard to get off the ground and then focus to stay in the air. She let out a big caw as I made a turn to circle back toward home. I looked behind me to see what was up. I didn't see the wind fingers trailing across the ocean, a sure sign of the wind gust that was coming straight at me. I circled into the wind and was caught in its unexpected force.

It's important to focus on what's ahead of us, not what's behind us.

I'm a reasonably skilled paragliding pilot. After I was blown back, I did all the right things. But there were forces I couldn't control. That gust of onshore wind was in the hands of Mother Nature. The ravine below me was at just the right angle to accelerate that gust straight up at me.

We have to be ready to change our plan when the unexpected happens.

So, what does my flight have to do with how you manage your businesses? Everything!

Our legacies jeopardize our growth. We apply status quo assumptions to everything from our product value to our customers' preferences to our market's directions. We assume that what we already know will apply to what's to come.

We forget to focus forward. We spend man-years collecting and analyzing past data, finding trends and "facts" we can use to forecast our future. We use our past to define our future, even as our world is changing around us.

We don't like change. We tend to stick with the plan rather than to adapt. That plan is safer than the unknown of change. The bigger we get, the slower we are to respond. We carry more weight, making it even harder to change course. We view change as a disturbance in our carefully laid plan rather than as an opportunity for high-velocity growth.

Either we're growing our business or we're losing market share. There is no middle ground in today's market.

Why? Because today's market isn't the predictable, slow-moving market we took for granted. What was true a month ago may no longer be valid. The amazing value we offered six months ago is probably not so compelling today. It certainly won't be in another six months.

A recent study of 163 leading CEOs found that, on average, one-third of corporate strategies fail.*

New market opportunities are popping up all around us. Yet, thanks to our tunnel vision, we can't see them. Many call it being focused. I call it gravity. Gravity is created when we hang onto our knowns, our status quo beliefs about our business, our value and our markets, long past their prime. As our markets change, we get stuck in their past—creating gravity that limits our forward momentum. Pilots are dynamic in their flight plans, just as we can be dynamic in our businesses. Pilots are also very focused. But they focus forward, changing their flight plans to reach optimum velocity based on what's happening

* Study by Forbes Insights and FD, in conjunction with the Association for Strategic Planning and the Council of Public Relations Firms.

they focus forward, changing their flight plans to reach optimum velocity based on what's happening in the path before them. They change course to capture better tailwinds, or to avoid the bumps, headwinds and downdrafts that could threaten their flight.

When you think and act dynamically in your business, you reach business velocity and then keep on growing. How do you become more dynamic?

Let go of the status quo. Release your corporate gravity, the weight and drag that hold you back and limit your potential.

Focus forward. Identify the truly distinct values that will power your future market momentum. When you map that value to growth opportunities, the sky's the limit.

Spin on a dime. Ride the dynamic winds of your market to high-velocity growth. Consciously seek ways to improve: make minor adjustments as needed, ever ready to turn up the thrust and to leverage an updraft or tailwind that propels you forward and upward. Accept change as a given and evolve.

Defy Gravity explores the dynamics of business velocity, that combination of value, dynamic response and forward thinking that powers sustainable business growth. It shares lessons I've learned in twenty years working with more than a hundred clients. I've successfully applied the principles of business flight to early-stage start-ups on their first trip down the runway; to companies seeking stronger velocity in expanded markets; to businesses that are spiraling downward. These principles work for any size company—from the smallest business to the largest enterprise, and everyone in between.

> You will either step forward into growth or you will step back into safety.
> —Abraham Maslow

The Art and Science of Business Flight

Our business strategies are, in effect, our flight plans.

We spend weeks or months defining just the right plans for our businesses. When we are done, we feel confident that we are well-prepared for future

FUNDAMENTALS OF FLIGHT

Flight is the balance of opposing forces: **lift versus weight** and **thrust versus drag.**

- **Lift** and **thrust** combine to overcome **gravity**.
- **Weight** and **drag** create **gravity**.
- **Weight** is inherent in all things.
- **Lift** is reduced by weight.
- The more **weight**, the more **lift** we need to fly.
- The friction of movement activates **drag**.
- **Thrust** creates movement.
- The more **thrust** we have, the more any **drag** will hold us back.

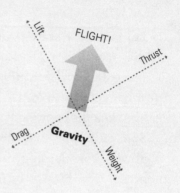

growth. The problem is that by the time our plans are complete, they're already becoming out of date. We're behind before we ever get started. Our markets move that quickly.

There is a better way. We can change the way we think about growing our businesses. We can move beyond the static one-, three- and five-year planning cycles that we embraced a decade ago. We can learn to think and act dynamically—in sync with, and even ahead of, our markets.

Let's take a look at how we can apply the fundamentals of flight to our businesses.

Business drag is created by the legacy of our business itself. One example is the mistaken ideas we hold about our distinct value. When we hang onto product legends, retain negative yet key employees, and continue along in the way we've always done it, we become less streamlined and carry more drag. That drag acts in opposition to our business thrust, taxing our forward progress.

Market weight is created by our market legacy. This includes the things we believe are true about the markets we serve. When we follow the wrong customers or, worse yet, the competition, instead of thinking for ourselves, we get heavier. When we hold onto our assumptions based on our past for too long, we become even heavier. When we carry too much weight, we can't be nimble enough to take advantage of market lift. We begin to sink.

Business thrust is powered by our value and differentiation. When our value is compelling, we take off and climb higher. When our value wanes, we begin to lose our thrust and descend. Defining our own value is difficult. We're too close to our business. That's why customers rule when it comes to understanding our most compelling value. When we listen to how our customers perceive our value and focus on evolving that value in line with their needs (and those of our prospects), we create continuous business thrust.

Market lift is created by new opportunities for revenue, profits and growth. Lift can be found in current or new markets. A key to maintaining or increasing our business velocity is to proactively seek out new lift—adjusting our course to soar higher and higher thanks to the updraft of expanding markets. For example, if we're selling business clothing to young professionals and expand our focus to include casual clothes and more, we're expanding our market focus to catch more lift.

Why Aren't We Growing?

Overcoming gravity is the first step to sustainable growth.

Why aren't we all soaring high above the market, enjoying the success we expected? The specific reasons are as unique as each business. But in my consulting career, I've seen four key issues that are inherent in nearly every business. Sometimes we overcome them; more often, we don't—at least not completely.

1. Our markets are dynamic. We aren't.

Each business and market situation is unique. That means each strategy is different. When we add the fact that everything in our business environment is changing faster than ever before, we have need for a very dynamic business path.

PRINCIPLES OF BUSINESS FLIGHT

Business velocity. The combination of true business value, market opportunity and forward thinking that powers us beyond gravity to attain business growth.

Drag. The legacy beliefs and behaviors about our business that limit our true value. Drag reduces our forward thrust and hinders reaching business velocity and continuous success.

Dynamic. The ability to adapt in real time to market, business and other changes in our business path.

Escape velocity. The rare ability to sustain business velocity for long periods of time. This results in significant growth to reach ultimate market leadership.

Gravity. The combination of legacy market and business behaviors and beliefs that result in weight and drag. Over time, gravity prevents our ability to reach business velocity and ultimate growth.

Lift. Opportunities for profitable growth found in our current and new markets.

Momentum. The forward motion that occurs when business value and market opportunity converge.

Static. A behavior pattern committed to the status quo, the way we've always done it and corporate legends.

Thrust. Forward movement powered by our true value.

Weight. The legacy beliefs and behaviors about our markets, customers and competitors that limit our ability to capture market opportunities for profitable growth.

Unfortunately, most businesses are not inherently dynamic. We're anything *but* dynamic. We create our plan, and then one of two things happen: either the plan goes into a drawer and the status quo returns, or we follow that plan, no matter what. When subtle yet telling changes occur in our markets, we keep executing that plan. When we do adjust our course, it's either by accident or after a big event gets our attention and we're forced to make a Big Bang change. Better late than never, I suppose, but not really. Continuing to follow an out-of-date plan doesn't help us target continuous growth opportunities any more than Big Bang changes and last ditch efforts will power us to sustainable growth. Following that out-of-date plan simply creates more gravity for our businesses.

We wouldn't fly a plane straight into a thunderstorm because the flight plan said we should. We'd change our course. If the tailwinds were better a bit higher and twelve miles to the south, we'd adjust our heading and climb to find them. *So why do we stick to our behind-the-times plans and focus, especially when dynamic changes would give us a much better chance for success?*

2. Our past success becomes a serious source of gravity.

How's that for a dichotomy? We learn from our experiences. We store that knowledge and apply it to our current situations when it seems relevant. We use our status quo beliefs and knowns—about our business, our products and our customers—to make decisions. The bigger we become, the more we weigh ourselves down with that status quo.

We collect and analyze historical data, identifying key trends and results. We project these historical facts onto our future plans, assuming the trends will continue; after all, they have before. We don't see our customers and markets move on to new destinations, flight paths and often, our competitors. Sometimes the market changes are so gradual we don't notice the decline until it's too late. The past becomes ancient history even as we're still following yesterday's truth.

We wouldn't fly a plane based on what happened even twenty minutes ago, much less last year. We fly with a focus forward, watching the horizon. Ahead of us is the lift that takes us higher, the downdraft that can send us spiraling downward. We also check every assumption and known before we bet our lives on it in flight. *Why don't we do the same in our businesses?*

3. We lose sight of our value.

Our products, services, and reputation are all facets of our value. We power into our initial launch focused on a specific area of market lift. We deliver our business value—our thrust—in concert with that opportunity *et voilà*, we reach business velocity and soar. But what happens when our value ages and we lose some of our shine? We may add other offerings to enhance our legacy power, to reposition ourselves and refocus on our markets. But our fundamental beliefs concerning our value most likely don't change. Our value is known, it's comfortable and we've been successful *in the past*. The problem is, as markets dynamically evolve, so do our customers. They don't see our value as compelling anymore. We begin to lose our source of thrust, and often we don't even know it.

We modernize our aircraft to deliver more thrust. We move on to newer and more efficient designs so that we can fly faster and higher. We've surely advanced far beyond the Wright brothers' first aircraft. *Shouldn't we advance beyond our status quo value, especially when the market has already moved on?*

4. Sometimes we are grounded through no fault of our own.

No matter how great a plan we have, external pressures and economic shifts can make that plan moot. The fact is some products and business models become obsolete. Our relative power and success in a market can change right before our eyes. Forces including government regulation, acts of God and technological issues that are completely out of our hands can ground us for good. Just look at the financial services vendors that offered student loans. The new government loans that came with new legislation basically killed this business market. The largest such vendors had wholesale layoffs throughout 2009. What could they have done differently? Not a thing. Their core business went away almost overnight, with little warning.

No matter what the cause, when we're grounded, we have two choices. We can choose to shut down and move on, or we can evolve and start over. The choice depends on how transferable our value is to other markets and how much of that value is still distinct. *Regardless, we have to evolve to fly again.*

We CAN Fall from the Sky

We can all think of companies that appeared to be soaring . . . until they publicly spiraled downward out of control. The following three examples really made me shake my head. The need to adjust strategy and plans seemed so obvious. They are sad reminders that sometimes we really can't see that big ridge looming in the clouds . . . until we crash right into it.

 GM and Saturn

> Saturn failed because GM's inherent gravity
> was too powerful to overcome.

Saturn was the first new General Motors brand in more than seventy years. The auto world hailed Saturn as the American chance to hold off more efficient Japanese cars. Saturn promised a huge thrust for GM, and GM put a whopping $5 billion of fuel behind it. Even that much power couldn't keep Saturn in flight. Executives competing with Saturn for GM resources argued the company already had too many brands, too many factories, too many everything. They secretly, and later publicly, undermined Saturn's success.

- Unions viewed Saturn as threatening to labor. Saturn was different, with its modern factories and robotic assembly. Its game-changing approach frightened them.
- Dealers were resentful of Saturn's big-dollar brand, funded by major GM investments. In their perception, they were struggling for marketing dollars, and this young upstart was being handed the market on a golden platter. Saturn had brand-new showrooms with all the latest and greatest of everything. There was no love lost between Saturn and GM's traditional dealer channel.
- Saturn's new designs used different parts from the rest of GM. That meant few shared costs and no shared manufacturing and parts. It also

meant little shared enthusiasm as Saturn was viewed as an outlier by other GM brands.

The combination of weight and drag created so much gravity that even with record market acceptance and revenues, the company could not overcome it. By 2000, Saturn was losing $3,000 on every car it sold.

With the federal government's involvement in GM, Saturn was deemed a liability and put on the market for sale. Penske's attempt to salvage the brand met with resistance; they were unable to finalize a deal to continue manufacturing Saturn cars with a new partner. On October 1, 2009, GM announced that it would end Saturn's operations within twelve months.

One has to wonder what would've happened if GM had spent the $5 billion on jettisoning its own far-reaching forces of gravity rather than attempting to launch a whole new brand into flight.

 Circuit City

Circuit City didn't fail because of a poor economy.
They were mired in their own status quo.

Every Circuit City strategy was based on the way they'd always done it. In a market that was shucking and jiving on a daily basis, Circuit City was just plain stuck in its own gravity thinking.

- As it was buying property for its stores in the late '90s, Circuit City sought cheap deals. That meant its stores were in out-of-the-way locations. Customers had to want to find Circuit City to buy something. "If we build it, they will come" is not a growth strategy.

- Circuit City stopped selling major appliances, eliminating one of the reasons people wanted to find them. Then they eliminated product specialists stationed on their retail floors, expecting less-trained staff to answer questions about more and more complicated electronics offerings. Contraction of value is not usually a strategy for growth.

- They were late to embrace the gaming industry, missing out on huge in-store promotions with the likes of Apple and more. How could anyone miss that opportunity?

- As we neared the twenty-first century, Circuit City didn't make its web presence a priority. Internet sales were booming; Amazon.com was soaring past book sales right into the electronics space. Circuit City was still building those out-of-the-way stores as buyers were shopping from the comfort of their own sofas. We have to look up from our plan and pay attention to our reality.

- Circuit City couldn't adapt to changing inventory requirements any more than it could to the Internet. As the business became more dynamic, it stuck to an inventory system from the Dark Ages. It couldn't manage its cash, its turnover or its bottom line. Business models change infrastructure requirements. Keep up!

By the third quarter of 2008, Best Buy, Circuit City's largest rival, showed a quarterly profit of $200 million. Circuit City reported a loss of $239 million in the very same quarter. Less than a year later, Circuit City was no more.

If Circuit City had looked up, acknowledged the dynamics of the electronics marketplace or the rapid uptake of gaming, or simply taken Apple's outreached hand, would they have dumped their drag and flown higher? We'll never know.

Everybody's Favorite Country Club

The economy didn't put them into bankruptcy. By following the competition, they left their market lift behind.

Flight planning doesn't apply just to big business. It applies to every form of business, from SOHO to SMB to enterprise, for a B2B or a B2C market focus.

Take my favorite little country club in the Palm Springs area. My folks had a house on this course in the '80s and '90s. It was such a wonderful place. The course and the community were straight out of the 1950s. It was a small, family-oriented gem hidden among the rapid growth and expansion of Palm Springs. We could walk the course for exercise and play with the dogs after players had finished their rounds. We could get a tee time easily on the weekends or walk up and play the cute and challenging little par-three executive course pretty much anytime we wanted. The food in the restaurant and the grillroom was plentiful, good and inexpensive.

Then new owners took over the club. They wanted to compete head-on with the big posh courses that surrounded this diamond in the rough. They spent millions modernizing both the course and the club facilities. New rules came with the new owners. No dogs, no walking on the course for exercise, no use of the facilities by the community. They tripled the prices for play and turned the restaurant's menu into expensive destination fare. A hot dog at the grill cost $12. Wow.

Today, that course is in bankruptcy. It's not because of the economy. It's because the owners changed course from a successful flight plan to seek the shiny market all the rest of their competition was chasing. They left their core value and market opportunity in the dust—reaching for lift in an already overcrowded marketplace.

That earlier club was successful because it catered to the local community. When the new owners shifted course to follow the other clubs, they left their best market opportunity behind. They couldn't compete with the larger, well-known courses. They didn't have the extra value to grow in that market. By chasing what they perceived to be a huge growth opportunity, they lost the favor and support of their loyal community— the source of the majority of their revenue. In the end, they didn't grow. They crashed and burned because they didn't focus on their own best opportunity for growth.

If they had stuck to their value and leveraged their velocity to offer more services and value in their own well-established market, they'd still be growing today. Instead, they lost, and so did the community they served for so many years.

We CAN Soar Higher and Higher

Market leaders soar because they continuously
and consciously adapt.

Market leaders focus forward, identifying and capturing new sources of market lift. They are passionate about their value, fueling thrust even as they jettison their drag. Sure, sometimes they get caught in a downward spiral: a market shift catches them off guard; an internal struggle weighs them down. But they pick themselves up and face reality. They accept change as an opportunity to improve their businesses.

Evolutionary leaders are always on the alert for changes that portend shifting markets. When they sense a subtle shift, they respond and keep moving forward. When it's a major shift, they throw their status quo to the wind, focus forward—and adapt. How?

> It is not the strongest of the species that survive, nor the most intelligent, but the one most responsive to change.
> —Charles Darwin

Evolutionary leaders:

Seek new sources of market lift. They serve their current market base even as they seek to expand into new and exciting opportunities for higher lift—powering profitable growth.

Reinvent themselves and their offerings to create new thrust and increased momentum. Whether it's a new product, an innovative service or a new way of positioning their company, leaders are passionate about finding and delivering new, or more finely tuned, sources of value.

Minimize their weight. They learn from their past, yet question every belief and fact about their value, markets, customers and competitors. They continuously test and adjust their beliefs, allowing only current market truth to guide their flight.

Control their drag. They keep perspective on their business. From legacy products to employees to the way they've always done it, they recognize that past assets often become future liabilities. They jettison that which no longer applies to their business, tuning themselves to soar higher.

Such evolutionary leaders aren't as rare as you might think. Responsive businesses that continuously evolve to soar are all around us.

 ## Nu Skin

Nu Skin grows despite a down economy.

Nu Skin has been in the skin care game for twenty-five years now. Personal care is crowded, it's competitive and frankly, the large vendors spend big bucks to stay in the lead. Plus, consumer personal care spending tends to map directly to economic conditions.

Yet in 2008, Nu Skin enjoyed record results. Their annual revenue reached a new high, $1.25 billion. That was an 8 percent increase in profit over 2007 and a 52 percent increase in earnings per share. How's that for moving beyond growth to reach escape velocity, even in the middle of a major economic downturn?

Nu Skin ignored traditional higher-end skin care market approaches. They sought and found revenue and market lift by creating and evolving their own best flight plan.

- From their inception, they adopted a multilevel distribution model, avoiding the competition in department stores.
- They grew revenues, reduced operating costs and made money in the worst economic downturn of recent history. In 2005, they began a business transformation initiative. They jettisoned the weight and drag from internal operations. By 2008, they had increased operating margin by 400 basis points while decreasing general and administrative expenses by 200 points. Read that again.
- Nu Skin focused heavily on product innovation to create momentum. They changed course to head right for an emerging market opportunity. Baby Boomer women were flocking to plastic surgery. We all want to stay young and vibrant, yet many women can't afford the $10,000

or more to maintain a youthful appearance. Today's economy makes surgery even less affordable. Nu Skin has the answer. It's unlike any other skin care option in the market. Introduced in 2008, their Galvanic Spa and ageLOC product systems are an affordable alternative to a facelift. And they work. I'm living proof. For under $100/month, we can get rid of the lines and sags and wrinkles that age us. All in the privacy of our own home. No pain, no downtime, no recovery. How's that for game changing?

 Southwest Airlines

Southwest soars because they changed the game, avoiding the gravity that's currently tanking the airline industry.

While every other airline in the industry is in trouble, Southwest continues to grow and thrive. Why? Southwest ditched the status quo.

Streamlined scheduling: Traditional airlines use similar scheduling approaches and fundamental rules of operation. The results are less-than-spectacular efficiency. Southwest threw that model to the wind. Their scheduling model is based on innovative principles that result in industry-leading efficiency and performance for themselves—and great on-time service for their customers.

Streamlined fleet: Airlines create extra cost by having multiple types of aircraft to service different routes and loads. Southwest standardized on the same aircraft. The Boeing 737—in three sizes—comprises their entire fleet. Think about the savings from that common sense move.

Superb service: Passengers consistently love Southwest for their exceptional customer commitment. They listen and adapt! We all hated the cattle car runs for the gate; now we have orderly boarding. When everyone else started charging for pillows, blankets, peanuts and more, Southwest refused to follow their lead even as their fares still beat almost everyone in the industry. Their employees are happy and well treated and it shows on every flight. We all benefit from Southwest's determination to defy gravity and maintain their business velocity.

While other U.S. airlines are declaring bankruptcy and/or merging with each other to stave off total annihilation, Southwest posted a $294 million profit in 2008 (excluding one-time items). $400 million of additional profit generated by special programs was lost to escalating fuel prices. Think about that. If fuel had remained in a reasonable price range, Southwest profits would have approached $700 million during 2008. As it is, they still made ~$300 million that year, while most other airlines were going out backward. Now there's a master of flight—pun absolutely intended!

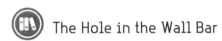 The Hole in the Wall Bar

> **The Hole in the Wall continues to serve the community that fueled its success.**

Remember the country club that crashed and burned? This little Hole in the Wall bar thrives two blocks away from that same country club. As the community around them expanded, the Hole in the Wall stayed true to their core value and loyal customers. Following others is not usually the best plan.

The local shopping center was modernized as part of community growth. A big western chain engulfed the locally owned grocery. The same happened to the local pharmacy. Chain restaurants with bars and fast food giants sprouted all around the area.

The Hole in the Wall was popular because it was a locals' hangout. The drinks were cheap and the food was as good as bar food gets. The place was comfortable and familiar. We could walk in there on any given night and run into friends from the neighborhood. Karaoke night was a riot; Saturday sports filled the place with good-natured animosity. The place was packed for the fund-raisers the Hole in the Wall hosted to support local community needs.

The Hole in the Wall didn't change in response to big-time competitors. They've changed as their community's needs changed—but they've stuck to their core value and keep dishing it up for all to enjoy. They've modernized the décor and upgraded the bar area with multiple big-screen

TVs for everyone's favorite game. They've added to their menu, offering daily specials at good prices. They've added new promotions to bring in new customers in high-growth communities springing up all around them, and they've expanded their advertising to include those same neighboring communities. But overall, they've stayed true to their community, and that community continues to stay true to them.

These three examples show leaders that recognize their best path to success. They chose to think for themselves rather than to follow the status quo of their business and markets, or their competitors. They identified their sustainable value, and then used it to fuel their businesses straight toward the most available opportunities for revenue. By recognizing their value and avoiding the status quo, they reached new levels of business velocity and profitability. You can too if you choose to think differently about your business and your markets.

How to Overcome Gravity

Defy Gravity is an evolutionary guide to high-velocity growth. It shares proven principles of business flight in straightforward discussions, bringing them to life through real-world examples. A Pilot Handbook sums up each chapter's discussions for a quick refresher read.

Section 1 delves deeper into the sources of gravity in businesses, including some of the common beliefs and behaviors that limit our potential as well as examples in real-world businesses. We'll also offer questions to ask yourselves as you identify your own business gravity in action—and eliminate it for your future flight.

Section 2 offers a guide to creating your best flight plans for sustainable growth. We'll learn how to identify and focus on the value that is your most powerful business fuel. We'll also identify opportunities for lift in current and new markets. Then we'll apply the principles of business flight to create a strategic flight plan that powers you to business velocity, including progress measurements and approaches to dynamic change that keep you flying high.

At the close of section 1 and section 2 you'll find a Flight Planner. Each contains a series of questions and exercises to help you take a sharper look at your own business and to define your path to sustainable business growth. The questions and exercises build upon each other to guide you in creating your best growth plan.

I recommend that many of your flight planning activities involve all the employees in your business. Focusing only on the executive team won't ingrain the dynamic thinking and continuous evolution that's required for sustainable growth. The more your employees understand and accept the need for dynamic change, and the more passionate they are about your evolution, the better your chances of success.

Openly promoting continuous evolution is important. Publicly praising initiators of change within your organization reinforces your plan. It also makes it difficult for the status quo to hide within your organization. That's why each Flight Planner recommends public measurement and promotion of the specific actions and results you require to soar successfully.

You can learn to soar the changeable winds that are inherent in your markets: riding the updrafts while steering clear of the downers; leveraging your value in available markets to reach business velocity. *Defy Gravity* will teach you how to do just that. When we reach for and embrace change as a continuous, conscious dynamic of business growth, there are no limits!

PILOT HANDBOOK: PRINCIPLES OF BUSINESS FLIGHT

1. **On average, one-third of corporate strategies fail.** Today's market isn't the predictable, slow-moving market we took for granted. Everything changes, faster now than ever before.

2. **Status quo doesn't cut it anymore.** We either climb higher or we crash and burn. Markets move too quickly for us to stay in the same place. High-velocity growth comes from a combination of continuous change and forward thinking regarding our value and the markets our value best serves.

3. **The most common reasons we crash and burn?**

    - **Our markets are dynamic.** We aren't. We follow our status quo regardless of the constant change around us. When we do finally adjust our course, it's usually after a big event gets our attention. By then it's too late.

    - **Our past success becomes a serious source of gravity**. The bigger we become, the more we carry our legacies. The more we apply our past to define our future, the more opportunities for growth we can miss, and the more gravity we create.

    - **We lose sight of our value.** Our value ages and loses its shine, yet we don't see that happening. We just keep right on believing in our best-selling product or service and its once-unique value proposition.

    - **Sometimes we are grounded through no fault of our own**. No matter how great our plan, external pressures and economic shifts can make that plan moot. Whether it's governmental intervention or economic collapse, when we're grounded, we have two choices. We can shut down or we can evolve.

4. **Market leaders soar because they continuously and consciously adapt**.

    - **They reinvent themselves and their offerings**. Market leaders are passionate about finding and delivering increasing value.

    - **They seek new sources of market lift.** They look beyond their legacy markets for new and exciting opportunities for profitable growth.

    - **They minimize their weight.** They break from their past, questioning every belief and known about their legacy markets, customers and competitors. Only real-time market truth guides their business decisions.

- **They control their drag.** They maintain perspective about their business. They recognize that past assets often become future liabilities. They jettison corporate legends and business legacies to focus on opportunities for future growth.

The Bottom Line. When we learn to soar the changeable winds that are inherent in our markets, leveraging our true value, we will reach for—and achieve—sustainable value.

SOURCES OF GRAVITY

CHAPTER 1

Change—The Anti-Gravity

Releasing the status quo is our first step toward sustainable growth.

We all know that change is a given. We reposition our brands, enhance our products, modernize our facilities and invest in systems and staff to improve our efficiencies. We update in so many other ways to stay hip with our markets.

With change comes opportunity for distinction and value, new markets and new life. Without change we stagnate.

Yet we don't usually change in the most important way. We hold onto our status quo thinking and beliefs about our markets and our business. We bask in our corporate legends born of past experience while we lose touch with our ever-changing market reality.

> **We create our own gravity by allowing our past to determine our future.**

Here are examples from my own experience.

A renowned software leader was growing at 30 percent per annum. A new upstart began offering a no software option (hosted) for businesses that couldn't afford the infrastructure my client's software required. My client didn't view some start-up as a viable alternative. Instead, this leader kept adding features (and complexity) to their software, chatting with their three biggest customers to define even more robust future products. Within eighteen months, the leader was caught flat-footed as this young company became a force in my client's own customer base. By the time I was introduced to this leader, their sales forecast had flatlined, even *with* the 25 percent discounts they were offering.

A start-up client was led by three key executives who had successfully grown two similar, yet more established, businesses. The executives

FAVORITE CORPORATE LEGENDS

- It's our biggest seller. Without it, we'd fail.
- They're our biggest customer. Just look at that revenue stream!
- To grow, we need to win some big deals.
- The competition has it, so we must have it too.
- He's a great guy. We have to keep him.
- Our product definition process works great.
- Our customers like the way we package our products.
- If we build it they'll buy it. Our product is just too cool.
- We can't win in that market, so why bother trying.
- Our sales cycle is a bit unpredictable, but that's just the nature of our business.
- We have to discount to beat that competitor.
- It's more effective to keep a current customer than to sell to a new one.
- Changing plans (or processes) will disrupt our business.
- We'll just have to cut expenses to keep profit margins.
- We can't grow in a down economy. Everybody is hurting.
- If we sell this deal at a loss, we'll get five more sales from this customer down the road and make a profit.
- Our customers want us to stay the course. They don't like disruptions.
- We're a leader in our market. Customers will follow us, so we'll keep growing.
- Our customers are loyal because we do so many special things for them.
- We know what our customers want. We're the experts, after all.
- The bigger we grow, the slower we respond to change.
- We all agree so it must be true.
- But that's the way we've always done it.

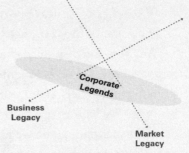

used their proven growth approaches as models for this start-up. But those approaches just plain didn't work in a start-up business that had *no market credibility*. Within a year the start-up was floundering. The company missed their most recent quarterly revenue forecast by almost 70 percent as I first met them.

The consequence of hanging on to out-of-date beliefs and behaviors is that our business growth—and ultimately, our viability—is threatened. Hanging on to the way we've always done it is the reason we get into a mess.

> Intelligence is the ability to adapt to change.
> —Stephen Hawking

What if Our Corporate Legends Are Wrong?

Corporate legends live long. But we don't always prosper.

Often we can't even remember the source of those legends, the beliefs that drive our business. Some status quo thinking comes from our own internal beliefs, some from external sources—like those business-school rules that are handed down from mentor to student. Many of those rules cause as much gravity as our own corporate legends. For example, the bigger we grow, the slower we can respond to change. That basically dooms us to the status quo once we're successful. How's that for a drag?

That's why it's important to always question everything. It's the only way to get beyond the knowns and into the reality of today's market. Be sure you always question your logic, that is, the "why" behind your thoughts, processes and beliefs. Keep digging deeper and deeper until eventually you hear one of two inevitable answers.

Because we've always done it that way. Some of our legends are still applicable to our present and future. But in today's fast-changing world, most legends are waning. Our markets move too quickly for us to hang on to anything from our past for too long. We cannot plan our future based on our past. By questioning our status quo, and the applicability of our assumptions to our present and future, we can minimize our gravity.

But we do change, all the time! We discuss what we see in our market, talk to our customers and check out the competition. We all agree on our best course. Then we create our product, target our market and off we go. There's one big issue with this approach. It's all based on what we know to be true. We discuss the market, agree to a course, move forward—all based on what we know. We follow the same strategy-planning process, listen to the same customers, follow the same competition and think in the same ways. We limit our ability to adapt by getting stuck in the knowns: from the way we think about ourselves and our markets to the way we approach creating a strategy. The result? We find out we don't have enough compelling value, or we've missed the big market opportunities. After we've invested our resources, committed to our course and either taken off slowly or crashed and burned before we reached business velocity.

Recognizing that what we knew yesterday probably doesn't apply today is critical to reaching sustainable growth. We can't approach strategic planning with our knowns and be successful. We have to test everything we know in the winds of the marketplace.

Throw Everything, Including Your Past Data, to the Wind

Gravity happens when false truths drive company strategy long past their time.

To successfully grow, we must release the gravity that holds us. And to release that gravity, we must first identify it.

The best way to ditch your gravity and focus forward for growth is to take a hard look at every single business assumption—including your facts. Take everything you know to be true and put it under scrutiny. Not just your own scrutiny, either. No matter how objective you try to be, you are still keepers of the status quo. As you evaluate your beliefs and behaviors, include a variety of perceptions: those from your customers, partners and prospects. Throw in some industry thought leaders as well. With their help, you will gain a clearer perspective.

Questioning ourselves doesn't come easily. Yet questioning is a critical element as we define our strategy for continuous growth. Here are some of the exercises I recommend for my clients as we begin to question corporate legends in search of gravity. Use these steps as the basis for your own self-evaluation.

The goal? Prove ourselves wrong. First, capture all of your knowns and beliefs. Include everything about your markets, target profiles, value propositions, SWOTs, products, materials, messages—anything that impacts your ability to grow. Then actively search for the facts to disprove those beliefs. Yes, look for the evidence that you are mistaken. Humans have the knack of proving things right when it's important to them. So don't look at why you're right; seek the evidence that shows your corporate legends and beliefs are out of sync with reality. Then you can make some progress on ditching that gravity.

Play Stump the Chump. Put together a brainstorming session and then ask each other off-the-wall and probing questions about your favorite truths. The goal is to poke holes in those same truths. When I do this work with clients, we make it a game, so we have a lot of fun and laugh at ourselves. You'll also discover new angles and opportunities to think differently as you're finding your blind spots.

There are no sacred cows. Question everything. Be tough, be fair and honest and most of all, be brave. It takes courage for us to look at ourselves with an objective eye. Especially when it comes to the beliefs that are the closest to our hearts; the ones that form the foundation of everything else we believe to be true. Challenge everything, ask questions, debate even your most precious facts—there are no sacred cows in business. Want an example of everyone's sacred cow? "They are our best customer." Go take a hard look at the reality around those best customers, being sure to look beyond the growing top-line revenue. You might be surprised.

Shuffle the deck. We have a tendency to analyze data and information in a repetitive way; we create the same financial reports, present sales forecasts in standard formats. Presenting the data in the same way—so we see the same things over and over again—is a practice that can keep us stuck in our thinking. So shuffle your data. Switch orders around, present everything upside down or backward, invert your funnel or look at yourself through your customers' eyes. Do whatever it takes to jumble your data and perceptions so that they become unfamiliar. The ingrained thought patterns will go away as well. You'll be able to see and think with fresh perspectives. If you think I'm being silly, try rearranging your Yahoo, Google or whatever desktop standard format you're accustomed to using. Then pay attention to the change in your perspective.

Ask trusted advisers. Spend time with your customers, partners and industry advocates. Share your relevant corporate legends and beliefs with them. Then sit back and listen closely to their responses. They represent your strongest source of market truth. Don't go to your biggest customer; go to the ones that represent the majority. The best perspectives come from your middle-of-the-road customers and partners. That's where you'll find your truth.

Ask not-so-supportive people. Check your beliefs with a few known curmudgeons in the marketplace. Don't expect to get a vibrantly positive reaction. You may find that their negative slants help you see your own status quo in a whole new light. Listen to their negatives, accept them as real in their perception and then see if they are really applicable to your situation.

The goal of these exercises is to let go of old and tired beliefs, jettisoning them to the wind while adapting your course. Sometimes this is the hardest part of all. It's hard to let go of the familiar, the comfortable, that creation you've loved for so long. But the familiar is often the baggage that is preventing us from soaring to growth and opportunity. You must have the courage to let go and evolve.

> Gravity is a habit that is hard to shake off.
> —Terry Pratchett

Take the beliefs and knowns that stand the test—along with the new ideas born within these exercises—and use those truths as the fuel for sustainable business growth. Chances are you'll find an opportunity for innovation and a new way of thinking. And isn't that why we're all here in the first place?

How to Use This Section

This section features the most common sources of gravity found in business. In each chapter I include an overview of a status quo belief or behavior, the business reality and the impact that specific gravity source can have on your growth.

I then discuss the questions to ask, or actions to take, to evolve your thinking and overcome that gravity forever. A real-world example helps clarify the impact of each status quo belief and associated behaviors.

At the end of the section, Flight Planning exercises guide you on your own search for gravity. Use these exercises to explore your own beliefs and behaviors, to separate today's truth from corporate legend. By consciously recognizing your weight and drag, you can jettison your business gravity. Once you ditch your gravity, you're truly ready for a successful business flight.

PILOT HANDBOOK: CHANGE—THE ANTI-GRAVITY

1. **We create our own gravity.** We get stuck in our status quo and corporate legends, allowing our past to determine our future.

2. **Hanging on to the way you've always done it is the reason you get in a mess.** Taking risks is not the chief cause of failure. Getting stuck in your past, resisting change as a form of opportunity—that's the path that will send you spiraling downward.

3. **You can ditch your gravity.** By questioning every corporate legend and status quo known, you can adapt and grow lighter. You have to be willing to throw everything you believe into the wind and prepare to adapt.

4. **Questioning is critical in defining your growth strategy.** Here are some exercises I recommend to clients.

   - **Prove yourselves wrong.** Capture all of your knowns and beliefs. Then actively search for the facts to disprove those beliefs; look for the evidence that you are mistaken.

   - **Play Stump the Chump.** Use brainstorming to ask each other off-the-wall and probing questions about your favorite truths.

   - **There are no sacred cows.** Question everything. Be tough, fair, honest and brave. It takes courage to look at yourself with an objective eye.

   - **Shuffle the deck.** Present business information in a different way. Do whatever it takes to jumble your data and perceptions so that they become unfamiliar. The accustomed thought patterns will go away as well.

   - **Listen to your markets.** Ask customers, partners and industry friends what they believe about your knowns. They represent your strongest source of market truth.

The Bottom Line. Releasing the status quo is your first step toward sustainable growth. Corporate legends are often the baggage that prevents you from soaring to growth. You must have the courage to let go and evolve if you are to reach for sustainable growth.

CHAPTER 2

It's Our Best and Biggest Seller

Successful products become like our children. In our eyes,
they are ever young, vibrant and desirable.

Why wouldn't they be? We have a great idea. We create, nurture and deliver it to the market with all the fervor of a proud parent. We sit back and grin as customers far and wide laud our creation.

Its popularity grows and we keep on giving to that winner. Our whatchamafizzle powers our business to its first big success. As our market share grows, we're thrilled with our oh-so-special child.

Then the revenue road gets bumpy; the future dims a bit. We conjure up the reality of our past successes. We know our baby is still our best seller. Sales may have slipped, but that must be a temporary blip.

We know it's our best seller, so we discount. Just a teensy bit at first, and then more and more. It's a subtle slide. We don't notice, or more likely we simply can't see, the true reality.

We see another blip. We surround our best seller with new products or services to keep it shiny. We even add extras for free to drive that top line. Lo and behold, it works! Our customers still love our baby. Just look at those revenue numbers!

> Even as we lift them higher and higher, best sellers may be dragging us down.

How can that be? It's our biggest seller; just look at the revenues. That best seller is our cash cow, sacred cow, the product that is our company's differentiation. Right?

Sometimes. But often it's not.

The products we love are often weighing us down, keeping our focus on waning markets, holding us in business models that are no longer viable. Yes, even in business, love is blind.

When our best seller is no longer selling without a lot of extra support, it's time to focus forward and identify our real value. We need to ditch the drag that the former best seller is creating and identify our true sources of momentum for our future success.

That's a hard idea for most of us to accept. We're emotional beings. The idea that we have to leave behind our best seller is just plain difficult. Often we stay stuck in the past, weighed down by that best seller and all the drag it causes, until it's too late to soar again.

Keep the Value, Ditch the Drag.

The key to growth is to identify and retain what made that best seller successful in the first place. Inherent in that successful product was a way of thinking, an expertise and a vision, an innovation. That secret sauce is our boost for the future.

Products are a demonstration of our value at a point in time. That value comes from many different sources: the distinction we provide, the expertise we bring, the difference we make, the experience we leverage, our vision for the future. That value also changes over time as markets evolve or change course entirely.

Moving on doesn't mean we ditch everything about our best sellers.

Our products, even our best sellers, must deliver value based on customer requirements today. When customers realign their requirements over time, our products must follow suit.

Look at That Top-Line Revenue!

The top line rarely tells the whole story.

You can bury a lot of mistakes beneath a growing top line. Revenue growth may signal success—but it's no guarantee. The thrill of the top line always gives way to the reality of the bottom line. The real bottom line; not the artificial ones—such as contribution or gross margin—that some businesses use as a fudge factor. In the end, the bottom line always rules.

To determine if your best seller is giving you lift or drag, answer the following questions:

1. How differentiated is this product?

Too often it's actually not distinct. It was, once upon a time, but it's not anymore. It's lost its edge. That once-upon-a-time value is now pretty much "me-too," with only minor distinctions. It may even be a bit behind in some areas, missing capabilities that customers really want.

Why is it still selling? There are as many answers to that question as there are companies to ask. Examples include:

- The reps are discounting to get more revenue. The company is okay with that because, well, it's revenue. Unfortunately, not all revenue is profitable revenue.
- Our best seller brings a significantly larger dollar value per sale than any other product; even a small number of sales make it look as if it's selling big time.
- Sometimes our best seller is surrounded by other products that truly are distinct. Its sales ride their coattails. When we discount the more distinct products as part of the package, that best seller still looks great on paper. The question is, how much revenue are we sacrificing from those more valuable products, so that our best seller can still appear as a winner?
- Sometimes that best seller is on the brink of its decline; we just can't see it yet. The joy of wearing those parental rosy-tinted glasses strikes again.

2. What does it cost to continue this product?

There are many factors to consider when we review costs. Some are obvious: the cost of the product itself or the delivery of service. Some are subtler and more difficult to quantify: the extra hours spent adapting the standard product to satisfy a customer's very unique requirements. To find the truth, we must sift the data and look beyond direct costs. Some of the areas that we tend to gloss over include:

Custom anything. When anything about a product is custom, there's more cost involved than we usually apply directly to it. That's especially true in businesses where the cost of services is applied as overhead across multiple product lines, based on revenue shares. Our custom biggest seller can suck up more service dollars than profits would suggest, thanks to that formula. The same goes for when we set a fixed fee for installation, delivery, or any other variable service for our best seller. The real cost of delivery and/or installation can exceed the fee. The more we sell, the more we lose—but the full cost may not be directly applied to our best seller. Do we truly understand these costs? In my experience, we tend to assume a lot about them. Not because we don't care, but because these are difficult to measure effectively. And because we've always allocated costs this way.

Special requirements. Sometimes the best seller needs a special touch: troubleshooting, special training for new people involved with its sale and support, extra service offerings for special needs above and beyond what other products require. Are we applying those costs directly? Just be sure these costs are in your best seller's mix.

Special assembly or packaging. Does your best seller need something special as it's assembled, packaged, or displayed? Extra time packaging, extra effort to manage, extra steps in the cycle? Every extra effort produces extra cost.

3. What are we *not* doing thanks to this best seller?

This is one of the more difficult costs to gauge. It's also one of the most important to fully evaluate and apply as we make strategic and tactical decisions. Are we strangling our future to save our past?

One company was investing more than 60 percent of their product development budget into a legacy best seller. The company built computer systems for the scientific marketplace. This particular system put them into the market and powered them to leadership. It allowed scientists to process certain complex data faster and more accurately than any system around, thanks to some architectural designs that were patented by my client. That value was still very important to certain customers; the installed customer base continued to buy more of these systems. But the number of customers who needed this system was declining in the overall marketplace. They'd found other, more cost-effective ways to analyze their data. The system's applicability grew more and more limited as the market evolved.

So why the heavy investment of product development dollars? It really was a cool product five years ago, and it *was* highly differentiated for those who still needed it. Frankly, it was also my client's adored baby. Their corporate self was fully invested in this legacy beast.

They were modernizing this system with new technology that still leveraged its unique value. They were also spending significant dollars to develop special one-off features in support of that shrinking customer base.

The problem? The company's future was suffocating. There were no extra resources to go around thanks to the resources dedicated to the aging wonder. A new system, developed by a different team, had game-changing written all over it. It offered access to one of the most rapidly growing markets in all of the computing industry. But they were slow coming to market and underfunded to boot. They couldn't successfully deliver the new product and invest in their future, thanks to that legacy beast. That new system would have generated some pretty significant flight velocity. They just couldn't let go of their drag.

4. Which customers are using it?

We have a handful of our best customers using this best seller. That sounds great! But in today's fast-paced market, yesterday's best customers may be tomorrow's losing proposition. How do we know whether our best seller's customers are the fuel for our future or the weight that brings us down? Ask these questions of your business:

Who are the customers of your future? Customers who bought your products last year may not be the biggest potential consumers today or tomorrow. Remember when businesses were the key buyers of personal computers? Or when games were for kids? Not anymore. As markets evolve, so do customer opportunities.

Does serving these customers cost you money? "Of course not; we've been serving them all along. That's how we made money." Yes, but as markets and products change, the cost of supporting that past weight increases. Have you checked lately to see how the cost of stocking those maintenance components, fixing product issues, maintaining that old man-ufacturing line, and continuing to train folks to support these customers is impacting your business?

What's the cost of customer specials? If you're doing anything spe-cial to maintain these customers, you need to track and apply those costs. Do they need a different version for every new version of your product? Do they need custom support for their unique situation? Do they need a special finishing touch? Every special is a cost. Count it.

5. How much are reps allowed to discount?

I am surprised by the number of companies that continue to incent and measure reps based on top line revenue instead of margin dollars. We cel-ebrate the $2 million revenue deal—a deal that in reality costs us money. I'm not going to get into sales incentives here. Just remember: *If you have to heavily discount your best-selling product, you might want to think again.*

Here are some areas to help you do a reality check:

Is every sale at a discount? "But everyone discounts, right? We set our prices so that we can discount—give the customer the satisfaction of getting a better deal." Okay, I'll accept that argument even though I disagree with this approach in general. Just be sure that the discounts are as planned and you retain the margin needed for product profitability. No slipping.

Are the discounts increasing? There can be a number of causes for reps starting to discount more frequently or for more dollars. Poor position-ing, poor sales strategy, poor product features, or poor market alignment to name a few. If the discounts on our best seller are increasing, something big-ger than price is at stake. Maybe the reps can't sell it without that discount. Pay attention before the discounts drag your bottom line down for good.

Do the reps throw in freebies to get the business? When we start throwing in the bells and whistles to get the deal, there's trouble brewing. Free installation, free support, and free professional services? They all cost us money. Yet sometimes we'll cover the reality with excuses like "We're adding value" or "The competition does it." Call it whatever you want; it's still a discount. Once again, ask yourselves, "Why are we discounting our best seller?"

The Ugly Baby Syndrome

One of my start-around clients, we'll call them Big Systems, designed computer systems in the high-performance computing space. These are the systems that predict the weather, send NASA into space, defend our country, and help Boeing design their aircraft. They'd taken off like a rocket in their market niche (no pun intended). One of my venture capital clients invested to fuel their expansion. I was retained to help create a strategy, positioning the company for future growth.

Although their sales were still growing, they were losing money. They claimed that to prepare for the huge growth just around the corner, they had to expand manufacturing and staffing. It wouldn't be long before they'd be profitable. Even though sales were still flowing, I smelled a rat. It was definitely time for a reality check.

Turns out they were building every system as a custom endeavor— from the ground up. Even when many of the same components were used across multiple systems, they redesigned a new wheel every single time. Imagine how much that approach generates in cost when your business really takes off.

That custom touch was their key distinction when they started the business; it was the fuel for their initial market success. Over the prior three years, they'd evolved from a start-up to a growth company, but their thinking and strategy hadn't kept up. Continuing to sell and deliver those custom best sellers was going to run them out of business. Why?

- The manufacturing process was no longer scalable. In fact, they were losing money on systems because of that custom approach. For example, when we added the total costs, they'd lost more than $1 million on their most recent $8 million system sale. You can't stay in business that way.

- The sales force learned to give away value-add and to discount as a way to get business. After all, their performance was measured on the basis of top-line revenue. Who cared if the deal was profitable? Almost every deal was at a loss, or close to it, when we looked past the corporate legends and into the reality of dollars and cents.

- Their customers knew they would take on extreme custom projects. They brought their toughest challenges—the ones the big guys turned down—to this small vendor. They pushed them to do the custom work at a low price. They also pushed hard for discounts and some rather one-sided terms and conditions. These very customers told me they didn't care if this vendor stayed in business long term; they just wanted the fastest system for the cheapest price. How's that for a valued customer relationship?

This company's ability to make custom, next-generation systems that actually worked was their core value. But their best-selling approach wasn't profitable anymore, if it had ever been. It was time to apply their high-value expertise in a profitable way—to repeatable and higher-margin opportunities.

———————

Market leaders recognize that their best seller isn't a specific product or approach. They identify their sustainable value as customer benefit, not a specific product. They leverage this value to fuel their flight toward new opportunities for lift. By releasing their drag and focusing on delivering their value in diverse forms, they reach new levels of business velocity and profitability.

PILOT HANDBOOK: IT'S OUR BEST AND BIGGEST SELLER

1. **We become attached to our best sellers.** They are like our children. Yet your best sellers are often the reason you're stuck in the status quo. If you don't realign your thinking, you'll crash and burn thanks to that best seller.

2. **Dig deep to find the truth.** The top line rarely tells the whole truth. Not all revenue is good revenue. Don't just look at direct costs of that best seller; those indirect costs are often the hidden drag. The more you sell, the more you lose. Always remember; in the end, the bottom line rules.

3. **Moving on doesn't mean you ditch everything about your best sellers.** Their secret sauce is the fuel for your next successful market flight.

4. **Be honest about your core sustainable value.** That's the momentum that will take you to flight velocity and continuing growth.

5. **Questions to ask about that best seller:**
   - **Is it really distinct and high value?** Or has it lost some of its market lift?
   - **How much is this best seller truly costing you?** Is this best seller truly profitable? Without profits, you are losing fuel and increasing your weight.
   - **What are you not doing thanks to your commitment to this best seller?** What opportunities for market lift are you missing because of your legacy focus? What new momentum are you sacrificing by holding on to your best seller?
   - **Who are the real customers for this best seller?** Are they really your best customers for the future?
   - **Are sales reps discounting?** Offering price cuts? Adding freebies? If you have to discount your best seller, you might want to think again.

The Bottom Line. Your best seller may be the gravity that drags you down. See the reality; jettison the weight. Then look for the sustainable value to leverage from that best seller to reach your next flight velocity.

CHAPTER 3

They're Our
Biggest Customer

A strong relationship with a customer is the Holy Grail we all seek.
With a win-win relationship, both profit.

Customers are the lifeblood of our businesses. Without customers, we have no revenue. Without revenue, well, we're not really a business, now are we?

Customers give us so much more than revenue. They're our sounding boards for ideas, our guinea pigs for new approaches. Their needs shape our future. After all, smart companies travel in lockstep with their customers.

Our best customers support us in the market with their success stories and interviews. They power us across the revenue finish line with new prospects—sharing their experiences and singing our praises. They test early-stage products and troubleshoot problems with us. Best customers are often our best business partners. They scratch our backs, so we scratch theirs: we give them extra products, offer specials, provide nonstandard hours or support levels. We spoil them. They deserve it.

Just look at that revenue stream. And there's another big opportunity with our best customers just around the corner. Even more revenue! Plus, we've been through the fires together. When we had that rough patch a while back, they stuck by us and worked with us to solve our problems. Without them, we wouldn't be here!

Our best customers can weigh us down.

Maybe that's true. More likely it's not.

Customers—especially our favorite customers—are a touchy subject. They're like family. We've been together so long, and we know each other so well, we couldn't imagine our business without them.

Yet every business is dynamic. Sooner or later we must all adjust our course or we will crash and burn. It stands to reason that some of our best customers will travel in directions that aren't necessarily compatible with our own growth. That's a business reality.

We've known our best customers for so long, and the changes can be so subtle. Over time the divergence becomes significant, but we don't always see what's happening as familiarity blinds us. We follow our best customers' road maps, mapping our own future plans to their focus and requirements.

That customer-centric approach works for short periods of time. Sometimes it works forever with the same best customer, and we grow together. But what happens when our best interests diverge?

Gravity enters when serving our special customers limits our profitability today and our growth tomorrow.

How Special Are They?

Revenue is not the best measurement of a great customer.

Nor is their longevity with our business or their willingness to be our public supporters.

Great customers are one of the most important assets we have for creating market momentum. Great customers can also hold us back. How's that for a conundrum?

There's a common business belief that isn't always true: We make the most money from our biggest and best customers. The reasoning goes like this:

- Our best customers are locked in to our products, our community. We won't need to discount to get their ongoing business.
- We may discount initially, but we'll get a better price over time. We'll make up anything we discount over the life of the customer, once they are entrenched with us.

Sometimes these points are true. More often, however, they are not, especially for those biggest and best customers. In reality, we frequently make less profit on our best customers. Sometimes, we even lose money on every deal we make with them.

Here are some questions I ask clients as we explore the reality behind these best customers.

1. How profitable is this customer?

Inevitably, the first response is, "We make a lot of money on them." Of course we do; why would we be spending so much time and effort on them if we weren't?

But what if that's a mistaken assumption? What if, in reality, they are costing us money? What if the larger they grow as a customer, the more money we lose?

"That will never happen," you respond. Okay, maybe not. But just to be sure, let's take a hard look at our results for each and every best customer.

Look at the discounts we apply. Are they standard levels, or do we dig a little deeper?

Are we developing special features for our best customers? Are we changing our product packaging or delivery methods to match their special needs? That's a drag on our bottom line.

Add the cost of selling to these large customers. Does that best customer have sales reps dedicated to them? If so, make sure their cost is directly applied as we calculate that customer's bottom-line contribution to our business profits.

Include the special service hours, that extra special warehousing or shipping or those weekly customer visits our field reps deliver—all for no additional fees. They are still a cost factor against our bottom line.

We offer extra value to our best customers in so many ways. And that's okay. We just need to apply those costs directly before we announce how profitable this customer really is.

2. How much revenue do we give away to our best customers?

Giveaways are part of doing business. From expert advice to special features or slightly tuned variations of our products, we give to capture and retain business. With our best customers, freebies can grow to be a significant and often underestimated cost.

Want a really simple example? Take my horse trainer. She is the most giving soul I know. She makes her living helping people with their horses and their riding. She also owns a ranch that boards around sixty horses at any given time. From her perspective, those people who board their horses are her best customers. So, when they need help with a horse, need advice about a wound, need a saddle fitted, have any issue at all—she helps them. For free. Because she charges by the hour, all that time spent with her "best" customers means she's continuously losing revenue. Sometimes she spends an hour or more with them. She loses revenue because she has that great big heart and her best customers know it. They don't mean to take advantage of her, but they do. I'm not saying it's bad to give great customer service. What I am suggesting is that when giving great service limits your revenue stream, you might want to adopt some boundaries. Define and communicate a customer service policy that creates and sustains a fair situation—for you and your customers.

Similar scenarios happen in all types of business. Our best customers know they're important to us. Sometimes they leverage that fact; that's just human nature.

They come to us for something extra: features, advice, special shipping and payment terms. It's okay to help our customers out. We just need to be conscious of the cost and know when we've crossed the line into a negative bottom line. We also need to make sure we're not being led along with promises of future business that never materialize.

3. What are we not doing because of these best customers?

There are only so many resources to go around. When we decide to use a resource for our best customers, we eliminate some other opportunity. The size and impact of that lost opportunity depend on the nature of the extras and the resources they require.

- Product development specials mean some other capability doesn't get developed.

- Services specials mean fewer resources for other customers.
- Free advice may mean lost consulting revenue.
- Special packaging means that we can do less for another customer down the road.

We want to be conscious of the impact specials have on our ability to move forward *and* to serve our other customers. We need to know when to draw the line and say no.

4. Is this customer representative of our next opportunity market?

Markets and businesses change. Our high-growth market from a year ago may already be slowing its spending—while a new and different opportunity is sprouting dollars right in front of us. When the efforts we expend on our best customers aren't applicable to our next opportunities, we're spending resources on waning potential. That limits our chance to tune our value for emerging and rapid-growth markets. If we're not investing in our future, we're limiting our growth.

That doesn't mean we stop supporting our past best customers. Anything but. We can continue to serve and support them as we've agreed to; we simply will limit our specials and draw the boundary lines more tightly. When we understand the divergence between our past and our future, we can define areas of overlap. We can then focus on those areas of overlap so that we can serve our past while fueling our future.

If we're in a more complex product business, customers often ask for special features or integration points. We often provide such capabilities as part of our updates or new releases, free of charge. Why? Because our best customer asked for them. That's a good approach in some cases. Those feature requests can keep us ahead of the alternatives in the market and give us differentiation and higher value. But what if those features don't map to our future markets?

The best option is to deliver the capabilities our best customers request that *also* contribute to our future momentum. Sometimes it's simply a tweak of that new feature to make it more broadly applicable. Sometimes we include additional capabilities to create a compelling package for that new opportunity. The key is to be conscious of our future as we serve and support our big customers.

That's a Juicy Carrot Ya Got There

One of my clients had grown at 40-plus percent year over year. They had an envious trajectory on paper and seemed well positioned for further market expansion.

When I looked at their customer revenue history, I noticed that more than 50 percent of their revenues came from their top three customers. The largest customer, alone, contributed in excess of 25 percent of my client's total revenue. That's a pretty scary business dependence, if you ask me. I grow suspicious anytime a "best" customer has that much power over a bottom line.

When I asked the executives about the revenue attributed to that customer, pride swelled their chests.

A couple of years earlier they had been in a huge battle for that account with their leading competitor. The competitor was ten times larger than my client. But my client won the initial Request for Proposal, which was the first of many more to come. Whoever won the first RFP had the inside track for all those future purchases. Since being awarded the contract, my client had been thick as thieves with the customer.

Smaller follow-on deals materialized as the larger initial project was developed and delivered. The margins were lower than expected because the smaller deals were priced the same as the big RFP. Also, the customer required something custom for each of the follow-on deals. They expected my client to cover those extras as part of the initial RFP. Since the customer had such a large deployment, they required my client's personnel on-site, at my client's expense. My client gladly went the extra distance for this big customer. They were all about keeping this customer happy.

But there were issues. Seems they'd had a big problem with the installation, and the customer had been pretty upset when the solution didn't work as expected. My client had invested man-years to investigate, but they finally tracked down the problem. It was in another vendor's product that was already installed. My client had to show the other vendor how to fix their own problem. But the customer was up and running, happy as a clam. That other vendor loved my client now too; they were proposing more deals with them than ever. Why wouldn't both parties love my client? Sounded to me like free development, free problem determination and resolution, free custom features and even free training.

The customer's next RFP was up for decision in two weeks—the next big step in the rollout initiated two years prior. My client's team had been on-site continuously, working with the buyers, users and management team to offer just the right response. The business was a shoo-in, and this time it was at a reasonable margin. Finally, the investment in this huge customer was about to pay off!

If only fairy tales came true in business.

The RFP was awarded to a competitor. Yes, it was the vendor that was ten times my client's size. They underbid my client by 3 percent. My client put their future on the line. That big loyal customer switched vendors faster than I switch toothpaste.

You probably want to look at this case as an exception. But it isn't. We all have to balance the 80/20 rule of business with becoming too dependent on narrow sources of revenue. The key word here is balance—and too often we don't.

Taking care of our customers is an asset. I wish more businesses focused on quality service and customer care. But we have to be thoughtful about what that extra special focus for a big customer means to our business.

Gravity happens when we veer away from our best opportunities for growth and realign resources in a less than optimum way just to please our favorite customers. When we don't keep our own success as a priority, we lose sight of our true destination.

PILOT HANDBOOK: THEY'RE OUR BIGGEST CUSTOMER

1. **Customers are the lifeblood of your business.** They bring you revenue, offer insights for new products and services, sing your praises in the marketplace and become like friends and family over time. Great customer relationships are the Holy Grail we all seek.

2. **Revenue is not the best measurement of a great customer.** Nor is the longevity of your business relationship or their willingness to be your public supporters. You have to look much deeper, understanding the costs of supporting and doing business with your best customers. You must also recognize the cost of the choices you make to support these customers—and the lost opportunities they entail.

3. **Your best customers can hold you back.** You take great care of your best customers. You follow their lead for the future, trust their advice on roadmaps and plans. But when your next market opportunity rests in a different path than your customers', you need to move in your own direction for success.

4. **Questions to ask:**

   • **How profitable is this customer?** Include all the soft, hidden costs, all the specials and giveaways and extra overhead you carry just for them.

   • **How much are you giving away?** Include the free products and services and all the advice and consulting you don't charge for. All those free little extras add up.

   • **What opportunity are you missing?** What resources are you applying to your best customers that could be creating your future success and momentum?

   • **Is this your best customer in your future or in your past?**

The Bottom Line. Big revenue doesn't equate to the best customer. Best customers power your success for today and tomorrow. They are partners in business, not best friends or family. If you're sacrificing your success for them, you might want to take another look at what's best.

CHAPTER 4

But It's a Huge Opportunity!

That big deal is just around the corner.

All we need is one contract with a big-name customer and we're on our way. We'll make more profit from that one contract than we can in a year on our current trajectory. We just have to find it and win!

We look for the perfect deals: the big orders, the custom work, the opportunity to serve the biggest customer of all. We wine and dine potential opportunities; we listen to the rumblings in the market for that perfect, and preferably large, contract.

Then we find a big opportunity. We're there at the right time with the right capabilities. It's a tough battle with the competition. But in the end, we win. We celebrate our good fortune with high fives all around. We've found the mother lode—the deal that will put us on our path to the big time.

But is it an opportunity for big success or big failure?

We'll sacrifice our strategy, forget specific goals, and even push our pricing over the edge, anything to win. If the deal is exciting enough, we'll lose money to catch that big fish. Just this once, we promise ourselves. We'll make it up the next time around.

Want a simple personal example? Look at what happens on eBay auctions as the auction time comes due. People run up the price, bid higher prices than they might find elsewhere, all in search of that great deal. We're always looking for that next opportunity to save big or to grow big.

There's something about that big sale that mesmerizes all of us. Whatever the opportunity, we'll step right up and take a swing. Even in small businesses we chase that big deal.

After all my years as a consultant, I'm inclined to believe that the motivation behind these huge opportunities is more about thumping our chests when we win than about business profitability. We get our chance to strut in the market, pointing to our latest nearly impossible feat and saying, "Look at what we did!" In that moment, do we really care if we lose our tails?

I'm not suggesting that we stop pursuing these big deals, however. Some do have the potential to fuel our business success. They offer proof of our value, entry into large accounts or industries and opportunities to shine in the market.

Why We Chase the Hero Deals

In the commercial space we sometimes label the big deal as a Proof of Concept (POC). Whether we're providing some kind of custom product features, a new way of packaging and delivering, new levels of service into previously untouched geographies or simply a whole new approach to solving a problem, POCs are a great way to seed the market or help us get our foot in the door. Yet all too often POCs turn into resource-intensive demonstrations of never-before attempted uses of our product, service or distribution.

In smaller businesses these opportunities give us the chance to get in with that big local business. These opportunities entail a significant investment on our part. Yet we'll latch onto the potential and do whatever it takes to fill the order.

In the computing marketplace, vendors fight over big deals with pricing structures and discounting logic that make CFOs cringe. We all know we lose money on these hero deals: on the system and on the ongoing support and service. Yet every big vendor will chase the latest, biggest, baddest RFP as if it were their only means of business survival.

How do we justify these hero deals? The logic is as diverse as the situation that brings them to us. Some of our common beliefs include the following:

The publicity will put us in a leadership position. That can be true, but only if we stay in business. We need to think about the true cost of this potential publicity and then compare that cost to other opportunities we might find from more profitable and less taxing customer success.

We can use the deal revenue to fund our business. This can be true as well. Finding a customer that will pay us for expanded development of products, services or even distribution is a great approach to funding. We just have to be sure that whatever special capability we're developing is interesting to many of our customers. Using big deals to fund work that only one, or a few, customers will pay for is not helping our business grow.

This deal will get us in the door. True as well, but aren't there other profitable ways to enter the account? When we set the expectations of specials and discounts in our initial contract with a customer, it's more difficult to return to regular operations and pricing down the road.

We'll make whatever this deal costs us back over the customer's lifetime. We discount heavily up front and offer specials to get the business. We know we can recoup those costs over time. But do we really? In my experience, it's rare when we do. It's more likely we set a precedent with the customer for our ongoing relationship.

Huge special deals can weigh us down. When we add the drag created by the realignment of our resources and business focus to service this deal, the impact becomes truly significant and often negative.

Choosing the Right Hero Deal

The key to success with big, investment-intensive opportunities is to make fully conscious decisions about if and how to pursue them. Then, when we do win the deal, we can thoughtfully plan our efforts to minimize business-wide impacts.

Before you pursue that next big opportunity, ask yourself the following questions:

1. What's the real cost of this big deal?

We can all determine the direct obvious costs to our business. Those are easy and generally straightforward, as long as we are honest about the reality of the deal.

But those direct costs rarely represent the entire drain on your business. For every huge opportunity, there are more subtle costs directly related to the deal. Be sure and include them—all of them. For example:

What are the true people costs for special product design and creation, specialized administration of the contract, that extra customer support you have to develop or the special warehouse management services you need to stock global locations? In my experience, we tend to underestimate these softer costs because we want that deal! Be sure and take a hard look at the resources—all the resources—that you'll need to deliver. Don't gloss over the cost. That gloss becomes your slippery slide into the red zone.

What are the additional costs of this special over the life of the product or contract? Hero deals are rarely point-in-time contracts. These deals tend to live over a longer period of time. How many special spare components or parts must you maintain? What kind of special knowledge and training are you required to retain in your people? What special processes are you activating that must be continued for the duration? What kind of distribution are you locking yourself into and what's it going to cost to support that channel over the longer term? The business impacts of huge deals can live forever, so analyze the full timeline realistically and accurately.

2. What's the opportunity cost of pursuing this deal?

This is my biggest rub when it comes to those hero deals. We work so hard to get our businesses growing, to focus on high-value opportunities. Then a big deal shows up and that focus is lost in the hype of the potential. We say we won't let this big deal impact our business, but do we really live up to that promise? Sometimes, but not always. There are two key issues to keep in mind here.

First: Be realistic about the drag this deal will have on your business. Then ask the tough questions. For example, in a product company, is it worth giving up resources for some months, postponing the product features assigned to them? Is it worth diverting your services team to support this large deal? What's the impact on your current and future services operations? Yes, you can add engineers or service reps, but you still have to bring them up to speed, so productivity is lost in some area.

In a smaller services-oriented business, the questions are similar. Can you really afford to invest huge sums to expand your consulting team and other personnel resources and train them for this specific deal? What will those investments mean to the rest of your business operations? Will the time drain associated with servicing this hero deal mean you can't focus on other customers or capturing new prospect business?

Measure the impact this opportunity will have on your daily business, your strategic plans, your future opportunities. Don't diminish the impact; you *know* it's there.

Second: Minimize the drag. The suction caused by such deals is tremendous, so wall it off from the rest of the organization. People will want to work on this high-visibility opportunity, which means other core work can suffer. Upheavals and problems can entice you to add more resources or change your internal plan to make sure this deal is successful. Be aware and thoughtful before making any changes to the plan. Every variation costs you somewhere; find that cost and apply it.

3. Is this deal really a fit for our business?

Let's say you're looking at a POC related to a much larger opportunity. Is the POC focused on creating and demonstrating a solution that you can sell over and over again? Or is it a one-time distraction that you really can't afford, cool though it may be? Will others customers ever want it? If so, it's looking like an opportunity. If not, then what's the real value to your longer-term business?

Take that big services contract for your small business, namely, delivering the customer's widgets across the United States—and maybe even globally. This new customer will take all of your resources and require you to add more channels. Do you really need those new channels for the rest of your client business? Or are they a one-off investment for a deal that may or may not be profitable in the long term?

Regardless of how much you want that hero deal, you need to be realistic about whether it is directly in your path or if it forces you to make a 90- or 180-degree shift in course. That's a determination every business must make. There is no set rule. Look at the facts realistically and objectively.

4. Is there really a long-term play here?

We all know that customers will dangle the promise of future deals, expanded opportunities and even corporate standardization on our solution. They use big potential to get vendors to bite on these deals and perform, even if it means a bottom-line loss. In some cases, customers will paint beautiful pictures of a rosy revenue stream that may or may not come to fruition. Take a hard look at the true potential before you jump to the assumption of future revenue.

But It Looked Great on Paper

Big opportunities pop up in a variety of forms. Let's look at a couple of different examples: one for product companies and one on a broader scale.

First—a big enterprise product deal. One of my clients won a proposal for a huge upgrade to a set of in-place computer systems. They would replace everything previously purchased from one of their biggest competitors. The deal itself was worth better than 30 percent of their annual revenue in any given year, and it went on for three full years. Wow! What an opportunity.

The contract negotiations were tough, but after they were complete, this vendor began to expand to cover the required product development, manufacturing and delivery specifications. Everything went well until the customer was acquired in a hostile takeover. The new owner decided to change some areas of the system design right before the initial delivery. It was their right, based on the contractual terms; this vendor just never thought they'd make such big changes at a late date. The original customer assured this vendor that any changes would be minor. Unfortunately, that assurance wasn't in writing, so they were stuck.

Those changes meant my client was late with delivery, and they also took a significant hit on the cost side. The new owner didn't care. All they wanted was their upgraded systems on time and on budget. When my client tried to negotiate a fairer payment and delivery schedule, given the major changes, the new owner suggested they could take legal action. They even threatened to expose my client's failure to the market if they didn't comply with the original contract.

My client had to pull out all the stops, and all their cash, to avoid litigation or worse. That single contract put my client on its knees. I was brought in to help them sort through the damage. But it was too late. We sold this high-growth rocket of a business to a competitor when investors decided to move on. That once-in-a-lifetime deal became their final opportunity.

Second—my smaller client in the wholesale world. They imported goods from China, specializing in home décor and personal items. They were growing at a nice and manageable rate selling to small independent retail stores.

A major retail chain in the United States wanted to contract with my client for their current merchandise, plus some special items that the retailer had identified from new suppliers. The retailer wanted my client to contract with their new suppliers, managing inventory and delivery for 100-plus stores around the United States.

My client jumped on the opportunity:

- The profit opportunity was there, and the expanded market presence was gravy.
- They got the chance to work with new suppliers in China, so they could offer that new merchandise to their current clients as well. More upside!
- They had strong relationships with their current suppliers, so they knew they could fill the increased orders for their current products into that new big retail chain, and they'd all win big.
- They had two warehouse centers so they could handle the U.S. marketplace more effectively. Good thing they'd added that second warehouse!
- They'd get the chance to operate in the big arena—and with a major U.S. retail brand.

It looked like a slam dunk. Then reality hit.

The new suppliers in China knew the big retailer wanted their merchandise, so they set terms and conditions that put my client in a tough position when it came to delivery. My client fronted the cash while the suppliers and the retail chain took little risk.

The new suppliers leveraged the demand from that chain to run my client ragged handling late shipments, complaints, extra tracking and paperwork.

The retail chain passed their deep discounts on to their consumers. Those discounts made it difficult for my client's independent customers to compete. The chain began to take business away from the smaller retail stores that were my client's loyal customer base. Because my client gave the chain deeper discounts, they ended up with less revenue from the same sales volume.

That big opportunity can drag us down.

Then there was the really bad news. None of the suppliers could meet the deadlines demanded by the retail chain. My client failed to meet delivery time frames because they were impossible to meet.

You can guess the ending, right? The retail chain terminated my client for failure to meet contractual obligations. My client lost business from other independent stores because of that contract, they lost revenue for the same volume of sales thanks to lower prices and they were left holding the wallet for those new Chinese suppliers who never delivered.

———————

Companies must resist the lure of the big time. We can't be successful if we chase every shiny opportunity that comes our way. When we focus our efforts on limited, highly defined and controlled opportunities to penetrate strategic, high-value markets, we can win. If a specific deal isn't the right fit for us, or if it asks us to step too far beyond our capabilities, we must have the courage to just say no.

When we get picky, we stay profitable.

PILOT HANDBOOK: BUT IT'S A HUGE OPPORTUNITY!

1. **We all secretly long for the big deal.** We watch for that one opportunity that will make our business successful forever after. We want it so much that sometimes we can't see the whole truth about that big deal in front of us.

2. **Big deals can bring opportunities.** The question is whether the opportunity is for success or failure. When you add all of the impacts that a given deal will have on our business, that big opportunity may not look so attractive after all. Then again, it may be just the fuel you were seeking. Dig deep for the truth.

3. **Look beyond face value and surface costs.** Hidden costs, special service and personnel requirements and expansion ahead of your logical plan can all lead to shaky results. Make fully conscious decisions about these opportunities based on all aspects, positive and negative.

4. **Choosing the right big deals means asking tough questions:**
   - **What's the real cost of this big deal?** Not just the obvious costs around product or service options. What are the hidden and long-term costs— the ones that will come back to bite you in the future?
   - **What's the opportunity cost of pursuing this deal?** When you take a big deal, you usually have to not do something else. What are the impacts of not doing this deal? What opportunity are you forgoing? What's the impact in the longer term to your business?
   - **Is this deal really a fit for your business?** Is there a long-term play here? If it's right in your sweet spot—great! If it's not, or if it's a 90-degree turn, you might reconsider whether it is an opportunity.

The Bottom Line. Bigger is not always better. We're all attracted by big opportunities. Sometimes that big deal can lead to big problems. You must be conscious and thorough as you evaluate these big deals. When they pass your scrutiny, you do win big! When they don't, you need to go find a better opportunity. They are out there!

CHAPTER 5

Our Key Employees Are the Reason We're Here

Retention of key employees is critical to our business success.

We all know the importance of hiring and retaining great people, from executives to managers to the worker bees who are the heart and soul of our business. Numerous studies have documented the high cost of turnover, so we avoid it whenever possible.

We work really hard to find the best talent for our start-up business. We keep right on hiring the most skilled folks we can find as we grow and expand. We carefully add management and executive layers to bring just the right skills and experience to our team.

We invest in their career growth and development; we listen to and act on their suggestions for improvement. We're especially grateful for key employees. They understand our business inside and out. They know our history and understand why we do things the way we do. When there is an issue, they troubleshoot for us. They're always there to go above and beyond to keep us up and running. We owe them everything!

But companies don't fail just because of bad economies, poor products or inferior service. Sometimes we catch a downdraft because of key employees—the personnel who we've struggled to retain. Surprised? You shouldn't be.

What happens when we outgrow our key employees?

Contrary to popular human relations theories, our current key employees may not be the best choice to lead our organizations into future success. A friend of mine once said, "There are no weaknesses, just overdone strengths." That thought holds true when it comes to employees. Paying attention to employees is a key strength; overdoing it can weaken us. Just because someone was a great fit in the past doesn't mean they are a great fit for the future.

Sometimes a company's growth outgrows a key employee's experience. An executive who created and launched start-ups may not be the best leader for a large mature organization. The people who helped us begin our business may not have the required knowledge to run operations for our expanded and very different business endeavor.

As we make changes, inevitably some executives and employees will hang onto the comfort zone—the way we've always done it. That's okay for a while; it takes time to get everyone on board with the new course. We expect that and proactively plan steps to bring everyone in our business along for the ride. At some point in time, however, everyone has to get on board with the new plan and the new direction. When resistance becomes a drag on moving the organization forward, something's gotta give. That something is most likely those resistant key employees.

That's a reality we executives and managers have a hard time accepting. Changing teams and letting go of old friends who are our employees isn't something we do easily. We want to be liked by others, and we don't want to make the wrong call. So, oftentimes, we don't rock the boat. We're afraid to make the tough, unpopular personnel decisions—until it's too late.

Business Is Not a Democracy

Key employees often fight for the status quo.

There can be only one plan. Everyone doesn't get to vote and decide when to change course or speed or altitude. There's one captain, one flight plan, one destination. We must all pull together for continued success.

Key employees are often viewed as the informal leaders of the organization. It's a poorly kept secret that we value them above others; just look at the golden handcuffs or special compensation clauses we offered them to stay for some lengthy period. These key players have been around forever, so they know how things should be done. But what happens when the winds have shifted and we're headed in a new direction? The status quo no longer applies to our business. And our key employees are no longer our future. Those golden handcuffs keep them in a place they don't want to be as we evolve our business focus—and we all lose.

Dissension in the ranks can cause one heck of a downdraft. Especially when our key employees are the cause. They smile and agree to the changes in public; then they return to their teams and continue to operate as always, negating any progress. They fight for the status quo—which is, after all, their source of power. Others follow their lead, and change slows to a grinding halt. In the air force, this is mutiny. In business, it's cause for termination.

Why do we hang on to employees who might be staging a mutiny? Reasons abound. If you hear yourself making excuses for certain key employees, you need to rethink their role in your organization.

He's a great guy. I'm sure he is. But if he's undermining your strategy for change, it doesn't matter how great he is. He either needs to come along for the ride or take a different plane. Niceness is not an excuse for an employee sabotaging your business decisions. That's insubordination (after a point) and it can spread throughout your organization.

She's been here since the beginning. Maybe that's part of the problem. Especially if you're steering a new course. If she's a vehement proponent of the status quo no matter what, it's time for a change. Just because someone has longevity with a business doesn't mean they get to mutiny. Long-term employees are fabulous resources when they follow your lead. When they dig their heels in, kicking and screaming, they're a drag you can't afford.

We'll lose people if he leaves. Maybe that's a good thing. If all those people are as resistant to change as he is, then maybe they're extra weight you don't need. If they are unhappy and can't see and sell your vision, you're no longer a match. Negative employees impact you internally and externally. No one is indispensable.

Then there's the unspoken excuse. Most leaders don't like to be seen as the bad guys. No one wants to be the heavy who fired poor Margaret after ten years of loyal service.

Popularity is not the most important part of a leader's job description. Sometimes the decisions are tough. When we don't step up and make the tough calls, our business and all of our employees suffer.

Raptors Among Us

So how do you know when it's time for an employee to move on? What follows are some of the profiles I see among my clients. Look for versions of these behaviors in your business. Listen to what employees tell you about the folks who are negative, but be sure those employees aren't manipulators trying to get rid of someone on your team they don't like. When you find these profiles among your staff, work to bring them on board. But set a limit. They must either show a change in attitude and beliefs or move out.

- **The Drone.** We all know this type. When a drone stands up to present their option, we all roll our eyes—knowing that whatever the majority wants, the drone will promote something different, and usually that something is based on the past. It's good to have someone share a contrarian viewpoint to our ideas: to work all the angles and try to prove us wrong. But the drones go far beyond that role. They drone on in the same voice about the same ideas, following their own course regardless of which direction we are going. If they can't move to the new business course and add value, they need to move on.

- **The Closet Revolutionary.** Everyone knows these folks as well. They smile to your face, agree with you in meetings, wave the corporate flag—and then go back to business as usual as soon as you're gone. They quietly stir up trouble in the ranks, suggesting in a worried tone that the new course is wrong. They naturally attract other folks who are concerned about changes, forming their own band of quiet revolutionaries who stick to the status quo and slow progress to a standstill. When you ask them if they have issues with the plan, they deny it; yet others tell you what they're doing. These employees are hard to pin down, but they can destabilize your flight. Dig deeper and find the means to win them over—or move them out.

- **The Blowhard.** This person doesn't agree with you and doesn't mind telling the whole world—including employees, customers and partners. Usually, blowhards are respected for some special skill or talent, so everyone makes excuses for their behaviors. *"Oh, you know; that's just good old Chuck."* Don't kid yourself. Good old Chuck can cause you more problems than your biggest competitor. Everyone gets to voice an opinion, but once the course is set, Chuck needs to get on board or go catch another plane. Chuck will tell everyone that the new strategy is lousy, even as he promotes his own status quo. Stop making excuses for him and add consequences for the subversive behavior if it doesn't change.

- **The Backseat Pilot.** These are executives or senior managers who second-guess every decision the leader makes. Sometimes they do it publicly; more often it's done privately. Either is unacceptable. Backseat pilots are one of the most destructive forces in business. I see them—hanging onto the status quo and their power that comes with that past—in every single turnaround client. All too often senior leaders don't want to rock the flight by changing out these status quo pilots. That's usually the wrong call. No matter how respected and skilled they are, if they aren't driving the business in your strategic direction, they are a major source of drag. If they choose to follow their own course—send them off to fly in their own plane. Don't let them crash your flight.

"Et tu, Brute?"

In their heyday, one of my largest repositioning clients had the best innovation ever; in fact, they were a leader in early computer graphics. Thanks to some misguided management decisions, they moved into more popular and less profitable mainstream markets. They changed course away from a rapid-growth sweet spot into a crowded lower-margin marketplace.

They had a loyal customer base. But those customers alone weren't enough to generate the profits they needed to grow. To capture new customers, the company drastically cut margins. And so the downward spiral began.

New owners came along and brought in a new CEO, a guy who had a vision. The company had shelved some of the slickest software ever. They could create virtual worlds, interactive games and power streaming video. They were smack dab in the middle of a high-growth market. Their true value and a very hot market were in perfect sync. Talk about an opportunity to reach escape velocity!

There was some internal dissent about the new strategy. Not all employees understood or appreciated the massive upside in the new business.

Meanwhile, a POC developed on almost no budget blew away 100-plus potential customers in early demonstrations. They were willing to pay big bucks for this innovation. But the status quo gang was staging a backdoor mutiny. Teams refused to support our efforts. There were wars over budgets and resources and details that should have been simple. It was chaos.

If your staff doesn't get on board, send them on a different flight.

The status quo gang demanded that their funding be untouched by this upstart idea. They refused to acknowledge the opportunity, sticking to the guns of their best sellers, even if they were driving almost no profit. The company fragmented, executive against executive. A group of execs banded together against the new strategy, refusing to allow their teams to support any of its efforts. They were all smiles and support in executive meetings, but behind closed doors they were hanging onto status quo for dear life. Managers and other employees followed their lead, quietly doing everything they could to dis and sabotage this new opportunity.

In the end, the infighting took its toll. All because no one wanted to step up and make the tough call to bring executives, managers and employees onto the same flight. The company failed—and a great opportunity was lost amid the internal battles.

Leaders must make decisions and follow through. Listen to all of the input, take the feedback into consideration and then decide on a strategy. That's why you get the big bucks . . . to be a leader and make the tough calls.

Hand them a pink ticket to a new destination. We may lose a few folks in the process, and they will most likely say bad things about us. But we need to get a thicker skin and step up. When we do, we'll give our business the chance to thrive. That's more important than winning that popularity contest, now isn't it?

PILOT HANDBOOK: OUR KEY EMPLOYEES
ARE THE REASON WE'RE HERE

1. **Sometimes we outgrow our best employees.** Just because someone was a great fit in the past doesn't mean they are a great fit for the future. Businesses change, markets change and experience requirements change. That means your key employees will need to change as well.

2. **Business is not a democracy.** One of the most common reasons for business decline is allowing dissension and diversion in the ranks. It can take time for everyone to adjust to a new direction. Just don't give them forever.

3. **Key employees are often stuck in the status quo.** As markets evolve, those status quo thoughts and skills may no longer apply to our business.

4. **Don't be swayed by these excuses:**
   - He's a great guy.
   - She's been here since the beginning.
   - We'll lose people if he leaves.

5. **Watch and listen for the employees who are problem children.** Especially the ones with these profiles. When you find them, either get that person on board with your flight plan or move them onto another flight.
   - The Drone
   - The Closet Revolutionary
   - The Blowhard
   - The Backseat Pilot

6. **Popularity is not in a leader's job description.** You must make the decisions and then follow through to assure that you have a rallying cry throughout the organization. When you don't, disaster is just around the corner.

The Bottom Line. Business is business, and no one is indispensable. Not even us! Make the tough calls and give up the popularity contest. Otherwise, everyone loses.

CHAPTER 6

But the Other Guys Have It!

Beating the competition is the name of the game.

It's a rare marketplace where competition doesn't exist. We have to win new customers away from their current vendors. We have to protect our own customer base against competitive attacks. Even in an emerging market, there's always some competitive threat. The enemy is everywhere!

Understanding our competition helps us create a winning strategy. We have to deliver everything they have, only better. Customers want the best option, the product with the most features at the best price, the best service that's the most cost-effective. So our experts evaluate our competitors with a fine-toothed comb, comparing feature against feature, capability against capability, price against price, discount against discount.

When a competitor offers a new product or capability, we match it. If they enter a new market, we go right in there after them. If we're in danger of slipping behind, we out-feature them, add more products to our current offering or discount our pricing. Once we out-feature and out-service our competitors, nothing can stop us! Whatever it takes to win, we'll do it.

When the competition gets a step ahead of us, we scramble to get one step ahead of them. It's a constant game of leapfrog, but that's the way the game is played. Right?

WRONG!

Competitive knowledge is a dangerous thing. Too much of it turns us into a permanent follower. Our focus on the competition limits our thinking. We end up following in their tracks instead of defining our own winning course. We obsess over matching and beating the competition. Winning against the competition

> Beating the competition is not the way to win the game. Serving customers is the best winning strategy.

replaces servicing our customers as our business goal, and we begin a long and painful tailspin away from the source of our growth—our buyers.

Worse yet, we use the competition as an excuse for every lost deal, failed market entry and less-than-successful effort. We fail and come up pointing to the competition: their new whatchamafloppy, discount structure or new marketing campaign was insurmountable. We must have a similar, only better, whatchamafloppy, pricing or campaign to beat them. We abdicate responsibility for our own success and empower the competition with our future.

> **Nothing we do that follows our competitors will make us market leaders.**

As my grandpa used to say, "The view never changes unless you're the lead cow."

Market leadership is not about being just like everyone else. Market leadership is about being unique. Leadership means providing special value in ways that knock our customers socks off. To find our unique position, we have to gather and analyze competitor information in the right way, from the right sources and with the right goal in mind.

Customers: Listen and Learn

If a customer perceives a competitor to be superior, they are.

All the time we spend on competitive analysis doesn't give us market truth. Reality comes from what our audiences believe.

What do we need to know about our competition to be successful? And how do we find the right information and then apply it in the best ways possible?

Ask the Right People the Right Questions

Focus on understanding competitive value from your audience's perspective. Find out why each competitor shines. That's why people buy from them—because of their value. Not because of their flaws. Once we understand the source of their value, we can differentiate ourselves.

Digging dirt isn't the best way to learn about our opposition. Besides, people are usually reluctant to share competitive information with another vendor, especially any negative feedback. So don't look for dirt. Be friendly and nonthreatening.

Value stems from many facets of the buying experience. Competitive value can be as simple as a front-door valet named Colin who treats every guest like royalty. It can be as complex as leading-edge capabilities combined with very specific expertise. Sometimes it's not even related to value; a renowned CEO who happens to be a friend of the customer's CEO. Don't be surprised by what you learn.

Gather input from a variety of sources. You can't exclusively ask your big and favorite customers for their opinions. They probably already agree with you, which is why they are your big customers. Their perspectives are important, but they usually don't give you an unbiased viewpoint. You need to go broader.

Speak with these three distinct audiences to gather competitive truth.

- **Current customers who also work with a competitor.** You usually have some customers who fall into this camp. Chat with some of your friends; then chat with some who prefer the competition. Focus on learning what they love and why they use both your product and your competitor's. Don't dig for the negative. Once you gain their trust, buyers will tell you the downside of the competitor—especially when they don't think you're seeking ammunition. Spend a little extra time building the relationship and then listen; they'll tell you everything you need to know about the downside of that competitor.

- **Customers of the competition.** If you can't find internal folks who have relationships, ask an independent resource to help find these buyers. Competitive customers will share a wealth of valuable insights, as long as they don't think you're putting them in the middle of a mudslinging contest. Sometimes I recommend that clients use an independent third party to work with these sources. The objective third party can gather input that you can't, simply because of your competitive position.

- **Prospects.** Find potential customers who are looking at your solutions and those of competitors. Be up front: tell them you want to learn so that you can better serve them and their needs. Ask them where you're failing in comparison to the alternative. Most buyers appreciate the candor. They'll offer compelling insights concerning your value and that of the competitor.

You can also use the power of social media and the Internet to gather insights about your competition on multiple fronts. Gather information from the market's perspective on product and industry acumen, hands-on experience, market savvy, customer responsiveness, overall knowledge and corporate viability, to name a few categories. Powerful brand perception is created through social media. Look for the buzz about this competitor on the social web. The truth may be easier to learn than you would expect.

What You Really Need to Know About Your Competitors

What you learn from your audiences about both yourself and your competitors offers a great foundation for your plan. Don't make things more complex by diving into all the trivia, examining every minute detail about your competitor. Focus your analysis on two key aspects and leave the rest of the details behind.

Identify their Achilles' heel. Everyone—including your competition—has an underbelly. The trick is to choose the weakness that maps to your specific market focus. Picking five competitive silver bullets that aren't important to your buyers doesn't do you much good. Picking the right point of focus can win the game. Sometimes you need one focus per market; sometimes there's one weakness that you can play across all your audiences. Be sure to focus; attacking multiple potential weaknesses to find one that sticks is not a good strategy. Explore beyond product offerings. Underbellies show up in the most unexpected places: areas of expertise, quality of support, their caring factor when stuff hits the fan, that slow delivery that gets slower and slower. You'll find out about all these Achilles' heels as you build trust with your audience.

Identify their sweet spot. Every competitor has one market they own. One of the strongest competitive strategies is to graciously give them that market space—especially if it's a complicated market that will keep them busy. If they can win hands down, don't try to beat them. Focus on other markets where you can win. Be gracious as you pigeonhole them into that industry segment or customer problem. You can claim a very different and larger segment as your own. If there isn't enough market to give them their space while retaining a sizable opportunity for yourself, then you might want to rethink your choice of markets. A limited market isn't usually the best growth opportunity—unless it's an interim destination on your route to a much larger segment.

 ## Listening for Truth

My client offered a software suite that automated business operations for small businesses. They focused on companies with around $10 million in revenue and under 100 employees. They had a great relationship with their customers.

I was hired to help with expansion planning. There were a couple of new markets this little vendor was eyeing. When I asked about competitors, they gave me one of the most detailed analyses I've ever seen: seven single-spaced pages of Excel spreadsheets comparing the three most threatening players. Two were well-known leaders—vendors who were moving down-market into the SMB space. The third was an online provider of hosted solutions. Thanks to this analysis, the client had allocated a rather large product development budget to remain competitive on a feature/function basis with these alternatives. My client believed these three competitors had everything and they needed to follow suit.

I went directly to the buyers, who I soon learned had a very different perspective from my client concerning these competitors.

- Buyers didn't view the large vendors as viable options. They were over-kill, and frankly, they overwhelmed the buyers. What kind of support could a small business expect from vendors whose bread and butter came from their big-name accounts? As small businesses, they assumed they would be treated as second-class citizens by the larger vendors. Sounds like an Achilles' heel to me.

- The hosted vendor wasn't even in the running. These small business folks weren't ready to put their precious business data and financials at some vendor's remote location that was out of their control. Keeping their data safely under lock and key was important to them. This vendor had little opportunity in my client's audience.

- The real competition was the status quo. Paper systems had been good enough until now, so many prospects weren't convinced they needed automated back-office accounting and inventory. Current customers mentioned they were concerned that my client's solutions were getting too complicated.

The bottom line? My client didn't need all those features they were adding like rabbits. They needed to focus on delivering what customers wanted most, that is, a simple, easy-to-use and manageable solution that focused on the specific features customers wanted.

We realigned the client's resources to bundle the simple solutions these customers wanted, based on a set of five use cases that our audiences agreed were their most likely application of small business automation. Most important, we stopped following the competition, adding all those features the buyers didn't want or need.

The results? We increased sales and margins in the new opportunity markets as well as in my client's traditional marketplace. We reduced the product development budget by nearly 40 percent and then applied those dollars to improving support and education offerings. The company grew around 30 percent in the nine months following our work.

———

Understanding our audience's perceptions of our value and the value offered by competitors is a key step in creating a flight plan for our company's future. When it comes right down to it, the only thing that really matters is what our buyers think. Customer assessment is the best way to learn the truth about ourselves and our competitors, as well as what we really need to enhance our future success.

PILOT HANDBOOK: BUT THE OTHER GUYS HAVE IT!

1. **Beating the competition is not the name of the game.** Knowing your competition is important, but it's not the winning strategy. Competitive focus is a dangerous thing. Too much of it turns you into a permanent follower.

2. **Market leadership is about being unique.** You must define your own value, creating unique and powerful distinction. Obsessing over the competition limits your ability to think and be different.

3. **Customer perception is what matters.** All the time and effort you spend on competitive analysis isn't that valuable. What matters is what your audience believes to be true. Listen and learn from customers and prospects.

4. **Competitive assessment that works:**

   - **Ask the right questions of the right people.** Chat with customers, prospects, competitors' customers. Learn about their positive experiences. Be sure to focus on the competitive value they see; don't go digging for dirt.

   - **Focus on valid alternatives.** We often get this one wrong. Ask your customers what and whom they view as alternatives to your offering. You'll frequently find that they see differently than you assumed.

   - **Do a market analysis.** Don't just look at the competitor's web page and product claims. You can't trust that. Dig deeper. Check out the buzz on social media sites and find out what the market at large is saying about them.

   - **Give a little.** Find a market sector, a problem or a customer profile where the competition excels. Then give it to them. Position them right into that market; sing their praises. Then stay away from that space and claim a different space for your own. Sometimes sending the competition on their own journey is a great way to eliminate competitive threats in your own markets.

The Bottom Line. Beating the competition is not the way to win the game. Serving customers with unique value is your best winning strategy.

CHAPTER 7

Figures Lie and Liars Figure

Tangible data shines the light on our best business route.

We've gone crazy over data. We collect more information than ever before about every aspect of our businesses, markets, customers and competitors. We analyze this vast quantity of data, seeking trends or patterns that will show us the path to success.

We find those patterns. Or do we create them? After all, we can twist those numbers this way and that to make them show what we want to see. Smart marketers do just that. We find the research we need to prove our point. Need to show revenue growth as a result of a marketing initiative? No problem. We evaluate our customers until we find that segment where revenue is growing at a phenomenal rate and use that data to evidence our success. It's a standard marketing approach. And it works.

So why wouldn't we do the same thing when it comes to data supporting our strategic plan? We decide on our course, based on what we know to be true. We find the data we need to prove that our way is the best way. When someone questions our logic, we proudly point to those numbers as irrefutable proof of our course. Who can argue with the facts?

My turnaround clients point stubbornly to the numbers they've used to create the strategy that they know is still the best. They've followed that plan all the way into the ground. When we take a new look at the data, we find that someone spun a number in a certain way or left out data to create their solid evidence of success. Sometimes, the person who ran the numbers didn't truly have the expertise required for a comprehensive evaluation. Regardless of the reason, the results are the same.

Numbers give us powerful guidance about a market at a high level. We can see whether it's growing or sliding, the potential volumes of sales and the relative size of an opportunity in general. But we have to use numbers with caution, pairing them with qualitative information if we want to make the best decisions for sustainable growth.

Operator Error

It's a natural inclination to massage numbers to prove our beliefs.

The fact is that numbers are not always objective. Raw data may be representative of what happened in the past, but people are the ones who perform analyses. People tend to spin numbers to get the result they want. For example, in computing, industry analysts capture sales numbers from vendors and then project their forecasts. Sounds good, right? Not really. Insiders know that the vendors all fib about their numbers. They spin them to make their statistics look better than reality and to hide any weakness. The fundamental basis of the research is flawed. Every analysis performed on these numbers is based on an inaccurate foundation. How accurate do you think that data is as a decision-making tool?

Numbers do have their place. But never, ever forget that anyone with a calculator and motivation can spin numbers to prove anything he or she wants them to. I can do it, you can do it; anyone can. Want some examples?

- A client showed me the margins on their products, which were a lot better than I'd expected. When we dug deeper, we learned they weren't using profit margin as a measurement; they were using contribution margin to measure profit. Since that number didn't include the cost of services—and their business ran at $1:$1 product-to-services cost ratios—that measure was inaccurate. Everyone bought into the contribution margin number because it made them look and feel more successful. The reality was that they were losing money on many deals.

- Another client showed me some phenomenal results in their sales pipeline. They were selling a fairly complicated product. Their close rates and sales cycles were unbelievable; the best I'd ever seen. I asked a few questions to understand more about this phenomenal success. That's when I discovered that, unlike most companies, they didn't put a prospect into their pipeline until said prospect asked for a proposal. That's a long way into the sales cycle before beginning to account for sales activity. Consequently, their sales cycles were unnaturally short and their close rate was high. These numbers were anything but representative of their actual cycles. When we changed the tracking to represent reality, their sales cycles were actually eight times longer and the close rate was 20 percent of what they originally showed me.

- A client's detailed analysis proved that their new target represented a $1 billion market opportunity. I knew a bit about the segment and doubted these numbers; they were way too high. When we examined the numbers more closely, we learned that an eager product manager assumed that every single customer in the segment could buy their product. Normally, that might be a reasonable assumption. But their product was only viable for the top 15 percent of the market— namely, the larger, more sophisticated buyers. The remaining potential buyers simply weren't large or sophisticated enough to want or need their offering. We resized the market opportunity based on reality—and changed course. In truth, their second-tier target represented three times the opportunity of the first-tier target they were initially pursuing.

These examples show why numbers are dangerous on their own. Especially derivative numbers—that is, the analyses we create based on raw numbers. Even if the raw numbers are accurate, derivatives are based on assumptions we make. If we have a faulty assumption, we have a faulty derivative. When that derivative is used to create even more derivative numbers, the impact of that single wrong assumption multiplies geometrically.

Would You Bet Your Business on Those Numbers?

How do you determine whether the numbers you're using are based on reality or on spin? Here are some checkpoints to use to validate your data.

1. What's the source of these numbers?

The first thing to question is the source of the data. The quality of data is only as good as the source. If anyone in the collection process made assumptions or massaged the data to meet their specific needs, the data isn't totally applicable to your business, unless the assumptions are an exact match to your specific situation. That's pretty unlikely.

2. Who is the statistical expert working the numbers for you?

What do you mean it's your sales operations guy or your controller? Don't laugh; you'd be surprised how many of my clients expect internal number crunchers to act as statistical experts when it comes to identifying market trends. Unfortunately, the skills it takes to run spreadsheets for sales forecasts or company financials are not the same as those required for quality statistical analysis. Stop spending money on research unless you're spending money on someone with the skills to discern the real truth from that data.

3. How applicable is the sample profile to your real audience?

Researchers gather data from vast numbers of buyers. We assume the results are factual evidence that apply to us. Care to know how many times the data isn't representative of our target audience? If someone chats with every woman in a rural area regarding a new face moisturizer, does that mean the results apply to your new line of wrinkle-reducing serums? What if 80 percent of those women can't afford your product and the other 20 percent don't care about their wrinkles; they like the way they look today? How valid is that data now? Big samples are the old-school way of gathering data. The responses of the right ten customers who match your target audience are much more revealing than the biggest survey results you can find. Those ten customers are answering your specific questions. The survey was designed for another company's needs that may or may not be applicable to your situation. Why would you rely on their data?

4. What are the assumptions behind these numbers?

The numbers we rely on to plan our growth are based on assumptions. So you'd better be sure those assumptions are accurate. We assume those thousand people who appear to be in our segment are representative of the other million. We assume a market adopts a product at a certain rate based on the trends we've seen in the past. That's some pretty thin air we're relying on for our future.

You must make some assumptions; that's the art of business. So base those assumptions on the future—not on the past. That's a big change for many of us because numbers, by their very nature, reveal a picture of our past. The trends we discover and the patterns we see are based on what's happened in our rearview mirror. That may have been an okay approach when change was slow, but not anymore.

Every assumption we apply to our data must be grounded in what's coming toward us. To match today's dynamic market, define your assumptions based on a forward focus. Use your market experience, buyer perspectives and expert input as a basis for the assumptions. Check and double-check them. Your numbers are only as good as your assumptions, so don't guess. And while you're at it, dump the SWAG method.

Solid, well-founded data is a great guide for defining your growth course, but it is not the sole guide. When you know your customers' businesses—their issues, their perspectives and their goals—you can make the optimum decisions for strategy and growth.

Market Experience Trumps Numbers Every Time

Whenever someone pointed to numbers that defied his intuition, one of my early mentors used to shrug and say, "Figures lie and liars figure." He followed his instincts and was usually right on. Why? Because he stayed focused on his markets. He knew their perspectives were a better decision-making foundation than any numbers from a market researcher. He taught me the importance of knowing my market and my audience, making strategic decisions based on audience directions and then using the numbers to fine-tune a course.

Numbers can't paint a complete picture of your markets. You also have to apply your intuition—that feeling that tells you a product idea has legs, a story is going to sell, a customer segment can and will buy your product. If you are steeped in your market, you'll know when you're on the right track.

But you do have to test your assumptions. You can't always just follow your gut and keep driving. If your market has changed dramatically in the past few months, your intuition is most likely based on gravity born of the status quo. Check in with customers and take an objective look at your beliefs. Make sure you update your intuition with objective market input at every opportunity. When you gain and maintain a level of market expertise, you can blend your instincts with quantitative information to create a stronger strategy.

Here are some ideas on how to get a better feel for your market. Begin to proactively include these in your business activities each and every day. You're already involved in your markets on a daily basis, so get into the habit of learning and listening during each and every interaction. You'll gain the market experience and perspective you need to balance quantitative data with well-grounded, qualitative market instincts.

Spend time learning about your customers and the markets you serve. We'll discuss this more throughout the book. For now, make a habit of asking questions that go beyond your own product and its application for your customers. Customer expertise is the foundation for a good, strong, intuitive market sense.

Study history, but don't wallow in it. Today's best strategies may just leverage lessons from yesterday's successes—*and* failures. Note, I said leverage, not repeat. Everything changes, so what you learn probably won't be directly applicable to your current situation. Modernize and tailor past lessons, tuning them to current experience. Most of all, learn to think and apply all those lessons.

One of my clients offered online services for traveling business professionals, making it easy for remote sales and services employees in small businesses to submit the expense and hourly reports required to account for their time and travel. We evaluated the history of that market to determine why businesses hadn't moved to automation sooner. That input helped my client tune their offering to be just the right product to meet market needs. We also studied the history of adoption of such tools in larger accounts. We learned from their mistakes and failures—and applied their successes to improve our own approaches. We didn't apply the larger company strategies by rote; we adapted the lessons. You can do the same.

Talk to objective experts. Too often we think we know everything we need to know about our markets. We've chatted with our customers, our partners and our sales force; we've read all the reports and done our research. We know what we need to know, right? Sometimes, but sometimes we've only scratched the surface. No matter how hard we focus and study, we may still have some remnants of our status quo, a bit of key information that's missing or the wrong impression that can limit our success. That's where experts outside of your company come to the rescue.

In every market there are consultants and strategists who eat, breathe and live the intricate details of that market. Use them. Hire an expert for a day to listen to what you believe, to ask the tough questions and to add important information you may have missed. You don't need weeks of analysis; spend a day picking the brains of an expert. You'll be amazed how much you can learn *and* how much time and effort you'll save when you plot a trajectory that accelerates your success.

Still don't believe in the power of trusting gut feelings over numbers? Here's a case in point.

Take Apple, an old standby for showcasing the power of gut-level strategy. How big was the revenue potential for PCs in education when the two Steves founded Apple? Education is a large sector, but it has always been known as the biggest discounting market of all—next to the government. No one intentionally targeted education as a key sector; you couldn't make money in education.

But the Steves didn't rely on the numbers or the knowns. They saw an opportunity to seed the next generation of PC users with their Apples by focusing on the education market. They ignored the numbers and trusted their intuition—and their innovation.

The rest is history.

The best strategies come from a blend of market experience and solid, focused quantitative data. Relying on either quantitative or qualitative aspects as a stand-alone foundation for our strategy leaves us susceptible to gravity: from our own status quo, from others in our market and from data based on our past. The worst mistake a business can make is to brilliantly execute a flawed strategy based on flawed or poorly analyzed data!

Apply your own intuition and the appropriate data, based on expert assumptions and analytical techniques, to create a picture of the future. Only then can you define the best strategy for growth today—and tomorrow.

PILOT HANDBOOK: FIGURES LIE AND LIARS FIGURE

1. **Tangible data is not always objective.** Numbers are collected and analyzed by people. People tend to spin numbers the way they want to see them to prove the points they wish to make. Anyone with a calculator and motivation can spin numbers to prove anything they want. Be thoughtful.

2. **Numbers do have their place.** You have to be sure that the numbers are based on reality rather than on the result of opinion or fallacies. Here are questions to ask to validate your numbers:

   • What's the source of these numbers?

   • Who is your statistical expert to evaluate these numbers?

   • How applicable is the sample profile to your real audience?

   • What are the assumptions behind these numbers?

3. **Numbers are not the best foundation for planning strategic growth.** Only by knowing customers' businesses—their issues, their perspectives and their goals—can you make the optimum decisions when it comes to strategy and growth.

4. **Balance quantitative data with market experience.** When you gain and maintain a level of market expertise, you can blend your instincts with quantitative information to create a stronger strategy. How do you keep the edge of expertise?

   • Spend time learning about your customers and the markets you serve.

   • Study history—about your market and other markets.

   • Talk to objective experts.

The Bottom Line. The best strategies come from a blend of market experience and solid, focused quantitative data. Forget the past; focus forward as a knowledgeable market expert to reach sustainable growth.

SECTION I FLIGHT PLANNER

1. Identify Your Top Sources of Gravity

✓ Review the chapters and ask yourself the questions included in each one. Make a special note of those chapters or questions that you resist; those are probably significant sources of your own status quo.

✓ Ask your team leaders and their teams to do the same exercise. Collect and aggregate the specific places that were charged with emotion—positive or negative.

✓ Now cross-check your impressions across your teams. Did all of you identify the same sources of gravity or different ones? If you found the same sources of gravity across the organization, you have a focused target.

✓ If you found a broad range of gravity across your teams, take some time and pay attention to how to eliminate the status quo. If you think you can eliminate it all at once—do it! If you need to prioritize—do that. You can only evolve in so many ways at one time. Just be sure you keep a wary eye open for all gravity as you finalize your plan and take action.

✓ Once you have the list of your own gravity, share it broadly with your organization. Also share the questions that everyone should be asking to begin to alleviate that gravity from your culture. And ask those questions every day.

2. Foster Change

✓ For each of the gravity sources you've identified, brainstorm ways to eliminate that source. Gather input across your teams, and above all, make it fun. Status quo is safe; if you're going to shake things up, it's best to use innovative approaches.

✓ Define three to five actions you can take to eliminate your sources of gravity. Post them all around the organization. Again, make it fun. This is about teaming together to grow, not making everyone depressed. Once you conquer the first source of gravity, move to the next one, then the next.

✓ Actively engage in supporting change. Don't just claim you're changing—change! Publicly note whenever status quo happens in meetings or in daily conversations. Keep it light, but note it. People will get the message if you hold your course.

✓ Leaders, if you drop back into the status quo, point it out. Publicly and strongly. Everyone slips in the early stages of change. Make it okay to laugh about it. Then change. Use yourselves as highly visible examples of change in action.

3. Check Your Progress

✓ Instill a method of measuring your progress toward change. One client started a status quo tally board in their cafeteria—with a goal of reducing gravity slips to a total of ten per week within three months. Everyone would add their marks for any slips on a weekly basis, and they all had fun sharing the stories of their regression during weekly team meetings. The teams even began to compete for gravity reduction. It doesn't matter how you measure; just be sure to measure. It's important for everyone to know you're being successful.

✓ Promote your success. My client with the tally board had a big party when they were successful. Rewards don't have to be large, but they do need to be visible.

4. Now, Do It Again, and Again, and Again

✓ You won! You got rid of all those sources of gravity. Now go back and keep checking for more. You never know when gravity can sneak up and snatch you backward. Be aware. One client instilled an anti-gravity team to watch over their business. Another placed gravity signs in all the conference rooms that anyone could point to whenever a conversation began to feel heavy with the status quo. It doesn't matter how you stay on top of gravity—just be sure it's a visible and supported company goal.

HIGH-VELOCITY GROWTH

CHAPTER 8

Continuous, Conscious Evolution

Big Bang changes wreak havoc on our ability to grow.

We achieve sustainable business growth when we first create value that matters to our markets and then evolve that value to meet ever-changing market needs. Notice that change is the key action in this formula for growth. We must dynamically evolve our business in mid-flight if we are to continuously soar.

"But we do change!" you protest.

Yes, we do. It's the way we change that wreaks havoc with our growth. Our idea of change is usually the Big Bang. We've all been there. The signs of problems are all around us. We just ignore them and keep pushing forward, knowing things will get better. One day we wake up and see a crisis. Then we decide to fix things quickly. We head off in a new direction or take a drastically different approach to our current flight. We change too many things at once and end up disrupting everything. In the worst case, we can crash and burn. At a minimum, we confuse the heck out of our customers, our employees and the market. We lose significant momentum and focus, and then, just when we get everything stabilized, we decide to change again. This time we don't give the new strategy time to take off and fly. The last time we waited too long to change, so we won't make that mistake again. There you have it, two extreme responses with the same result.

"But we can't watch over every strategic detail of our business. We'll never get anything done!"

That's true, but only because our traditional strategic process is unwieldy. That's why we hold annual strategy meetings: we can't afford to think strategically more than once a year thanks to the distraction strategic planning creates. We spend weeks preparing for the strategy meeting, show up with our plans and then spend more time blending all the plans together from the diverse facets of our business. It's disruptive for a period of time, but then we move back to business operations according to the new plan—sort of. It's more likely that we hang onto the way we've always done it. It's human nature. And, we wait until the next planning meeting to adjust our course again.

There's a better way to reach sustainable growth.

We attain sustainable growth when we accept that change is a given, approaching strategy with an eye toward continuous small evolutions instead of those Big Bang changes. We move forward in an aligned and less disruptive fashion. We recognize what works and let go of what doesn't, implementing quick yet powerful iterations of our strategy. We release our status quo before it becomes gravity, evolving as we go—all the while climbing higher and higher.

In flight, pilots don't take off and head straight for their destination without monitoring and realigning their route when necessary. They continuously check their course, speed, altitude and other key elements, adjusting as needed for an optimal flight.

We can do the same in our businesses. Once we have a strategic vision and plan, we can treat it as a living, breathing map of our flight. When we see an issue or an opportunity, we can make minor adjustments to optimize our plan, even as we maintain our overall stability. That's a much more effective approach than the Big Bang change, isn't it?

Continuous Evolution Brings Sustainable Growth

We're either growing or we're contracting.

When we evolve to sync with our markets, we grow. When we hang on to the past or even to today, we stagnate. There is no static anything. The opportunity for "good enough" that we enjoyed for decades doesn't exist in today's world. Remember when flat revenue and decent profit margins meant safety? That good old middle of the road doesn't cut it anymore.

Why?

The value and markets that fueled our growth become gravity over time. As our markets accelerate, so does this pattern. Either we evolve and rise with new value and opportunity or we fall to overwhelming gravity.

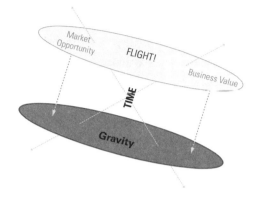

Ever-Evolving Lift and Thrust

Great companies realign continuously to create compelling value in high-opportunity markets. They leverage their enhanced value to enter new and growth-oriented markets, while also evolving to meet the needs of their current yet ever-changing customers.

How to Use This Section

This section helps you apply the principles of flight to your business.

In chapter 9, we'll discuss value—the fuel that powers business momentum. We'll examine the three facets of your Value Mix: company, product and market value. Then we'll explore examples in real-world business practice and examine how to apply each in diverse situations.

Lift and thrust become weight and drag over time.

You'll learn how to identify your own Value Mix in chapter 10. Real-world case studies and exercises bring the lessons from chapter 9 to life in your own business reality.

In chapter 11 we'll explore the horizon of opportunity that is present in every business. We'll examine the market segments that comprise your Opportunity Horizon, discussing how each segment comes into play depending on your specific business situation.

You'll learn how to create your own Opportunity Horizon in chapter 12. You'll capture and prioritize your best opportunities for market lift, then map those opportunities to your value, focusing for sustainable growth.

Chapter 13 brings it all together, mapping business value to market opportunity and available resources, creating a strategic flight plan. You'll also learn how to identify priority routes and create test flights to better fuel your growth.

Waypoints and trim tabs, key tools for monitoring and managing growth, are introduced in chapter 14. We'll review examples and ways to use these tools in a variety of real-world scenarios.

Chapter 15 applies the art of strategy to real-world strategy through case studies representing a variety of business situations. Each of these scenarios demonstrates a unique form of situational thinking, offering samples of diverse thinking to expand your own thought processes.

The section ends with a series of flight-planning exercises. This Flight Planner guides you as you identify optimum value and market opportunities, create a strategic flight plan, measure progress and evolve to capture sustainable growth.

CHAPTER 9

The Dynamics of Value

Winning value is not created by volume; it's created by focus.

Value is an ever-changing blend of tangible and intangible aspects that compel customers to buy from us. Value powers us to business velocity. Yet value is a special blend for every company. In our dynamic markets, we must identify and consciously evolve our value to meet the changing needs of our customers if we are to grow.

That doesn't mean we grab onto every single aspect of the value we might offer, running out to develop and promote it to the world. Anything but. That kind of scattershot approach is destined for failure.

Instead, we identify our Value Mix—those key elements of value that make us compelling and distinct. In flight, the more powerful our engines, the stronger our thrust. In business, the stronger our Value Mix, the more powerful our fuel for growth.

The Value Mix

Our Value Mix is the intersection of a company's most differentiated strengths with distinct consumer/buyer demand.

We use our Value Mix to guide the evolution of our business for sustainable and profitable growth. Defining a powerful Value Mix and then advancing that Value Mix in a focused way is the way to create distinction and growth. Our Value Mix represents the fuel that creates forward thrust for our business. Once we define our Value Mix, we can map it to our market opportunities to determine our best course.

The Three Segments of Value

The right Value Mix reflects the strengths of our company, our products and our market position. Within each aspect of our value, we have both core value and segment value.

First let's explore company, product and market value. Then we'll discuss how core and segment value relate to each of these aspects of our Value Mix. In the next chapter, we'll examine the process for defining these values for your company.

Company Value

> **Our company is more than a building or a brand,
> a product or a service.**

To define our best company value, we have to think beyond our offerings, examining our value independent of any specific product. Products come and go. Our company value must remain true, even as our product offerings change over time.

Companies have personalities and cultures. Think about one of the companies you admire in your business or personal life. What value do you associate with that company? What do you feel when you think about that company's value? What's your expectation of that company?

Chances are you aren't thinking about their products or services alone. There is so much more to a company than its products! There are tangible aspects of a company's position: market shares and profitability, the number of customers and longevity in the business. Then there are the intangible aspects: the company's expertise, the smiling faces that greet customers and the fact that for generations families have been buying that same brand.

Company value is so powerful it can see us through the tough times. Just look at General Motors. GM took some wrong turns and missed a few major opportunities. Yet it's attempting a new growth flight, and people are willing to support that endeavor with their dollars. Partially because of the automobiles GM is producing, but more so because of the power of the GM brand—handed down from generation to generation as the mark of trusted value.

Product Value

Product value goes far beyond features.

Product value comes from a key problem we solve for a customer, our deep expertise, simplicity of use or our attractive pricing—just to name a few examples. (For succinctness, I am using the term "product value" to include values from products, services, expertise or solutions.) It's the benefit customers perceive we bring—in their business and professional lives and in their personal lives.

Product value isn't about features or capabilities; it's the results customers get when they use the product. The most important question to ask, then, is, "So What? What happens for our customer?"

Why? Because competitors can claim superiority in feature-to-feature comparisons. It's as easy as adding a feature to a list and claiming it's already there. Distinct value comes from the benefits derived by our customer. When we have proof of that value, it's much more difficult for the competition to "me-too" us with rhetoric and promises.

Determining our true product value helps us stay focused on our strong suits while forming flexible boundaries for our product evolution. We remain focused when we expand our product lines within the boundaries of our value, being thoughtful before we jump to a more diversified product area that's outside our boundaries. We don't want to confuse our customers, our markets or ourselves.

Focus is the key to sustainable product value, just as it is for sustainable growth. Trying to do too much, to reach beyond our value into areas where we're just not that distinct or credible, will throttle our growth every time.

Market Value

Market value is the most powerful of all values.

Market value is a strong, yet often overlooked, aspect of our overall Value Mix. Market value is based on our oomph—that is, the power we enjoy in certain market segments based on evidence of our customers' success or on word-of-mouth credibility. Our audiences and supporters create our market value.

When our buyers and/or our partners are successful, we create market value. When a number of leading players in a market segment are our customers, we have value in that segment. When we've been recognized for years as the market leader in a certain industry, we have market value in that industry.

The key to market value is making other people successful. Sure, what we do in the form of market share, growth rates and sheer brand presence is important. But I view those aspects as evidence of company value. The true measure of market value is the power of our support in our markets.

For every customer or partner success that we enable, we attain more than just revenue fuel; we capture market recommendations. When customers speak highly of us, when partners share our value with their own audiences, when industry experts point to our value—we grow in market value and power.

Core and Segment Value

Within each of the three facets of our Value Mix, we identify both core and segment value.

- Core values remain the same across markets and audiences, and they evolve much more slowly than do segment values.
- Segment values apply to specific segments of our audience. Segment values can be focused on specific industries, age groups, job descriptions—whatever makes sense in your situation.

We combine core and segment values to create distinct and compelling values for each of our audiences. By staying true to our core values, we maintain our focus over time. By supplementing these core values with audience-specific differentiation, we tune our value to meet diverse buyer needs and perceptions.

Core value is the essence of our business as perceived by all of our audiences. Often it's the reason we began our business in the first place. Core value is a thread that blends with each and every other value we offer. Core value isn't complex; it's straightforward and concise. It is often emotional or personal—even in B2B markets. For example:

- Lexus is synonymous with quality products and a great customer experience.
- The *New York Times* is synonymous with hard-hitting news and thought-provoking editorials.
- The IRS is synonymous with taxes and a yearly groan.

Core value is not the positioning we promote in our marketing and sales efforts. For example, solving a workforce automation problem or cleaning a red wine stain out of that white tablecloth better than anyone else is not core value. Those are product-specific features and benefits that may be tied to product core or segment value. Although they are important to our marketing and sales, they don't reflect the singular focus that will keep us true to our course.

Focusing on our core value is one key aspect of growth. Even as we expand and evolve, we don't want to abandon our core value without serious thought. We can stunt our growth if we make those kinds of drastic course corrections.

For example, if we're delivering the world's leading golf clubs and our core value is to help golfers lower their score, evolving to provide longer-distance or more accurate golf balls is in alignment with our core value. Clothing might be in alignment as well, although it's more of a stretch, considering the difference in manufacturing and skill sets that are required. Deciding to begin to manufacture and sell golf carts is a major right turn—and not necessarily in our best interest. Even though that product is still about golf, it's not in line with our core value: golf carts do not lower scores. It's also a different product manufacturing focus that requires a whole new focus for our distribution channels and services. Perhaps it's an opportunity for partnering, but not for our direct focus. It's more likely to confuse our buyers and our business operations, causing more problems than opportunity.

Segment values give us a turbo-boost in specific market segments or audiences. We evolve to keep these values aligned directly with the needs of our customers.

Segment value is our distinction as perceived by markets and customers, a topic we will discuss in greater detail in the next chapter. Segment value comes from a wide variety of benefits customers derive when working

Characteristics of Core and Segment Value

	IS	IS NOT
Core Value	Consistent across audiences	Different for diverse audiences
	Complementary to other values	Our marketing slogans
	Emotional/personal in nature	Changeable on short notice
	Distinct across time	Only tangible facts
	Tied to our brand	Confusing to our audiences
Segment Value	Specific to distinct audiences	Features or feeds n speeds
	Tied to the benefits our audience receives	The same across all markets
	Combinable with core value	Based on our opinions
	Evolving with our markets	Standalone in a unique direction
	Clear and concise	Static in nature

with us: for instance, that collaborative capability no other vendor can deliver, or that simple stain remover that housewives love.

I usually limit segment value to between one and three points of focus for each audience. If we can't identify concise, focused value, how can we hope to communicate it to those who want it?

I know what you're thinking: "But we have more than three value positions in each audience; we have multiple product lines and great features." That's why you first gather feedback and then begin the process of combining and elevating the value points to find a key value thread for each audience. Ideally, you'll have one per segment; that's the best case. Remember, throughout this process we're focusing.

Sometimes you need multiple threads of segment value, and that's okay. Don't get hung up on having a single segment value for each market. Focus on finding the right segment value. Just don't let yourself off the clarity hook by succumbing to the more-is-better approach when defining strategic value. You'll waste money and resources as you spin around evolving every aspect of your business that seems valuable. Over time, such actions create gravity. They confuse and fragment our focus and limit our growth. Less is more. Dig deep. If you do need two or more values, then add them. Just don't take the quick approach and throw more value than necessary into the mix.

Examples of segment value are all around us.

- That speedy touch interface on my iPhone offers segment value. It lets me quickly access volumes of information by easily thumbing through the pages. That segment value is in sync with Apple's core value—ease of use.

- Integrated services (voice, data networking, security, email and more) for a business communications customer are segment value. These also stay in sync with a communication company's core value—dependable, simple access to the networking aspects I need for my business.

- Healthy food menus are a segment value for fast food chains. They compel a submarket—healthy parents—to share a meal with their kids at the drive through. They are also in sync with any fast food chain's core value—providing, um, fast food.

THE VALUE MIX MODEL

When we evolve to enhance our Value Mix as markets evolve, we grow. If we focus on value that isn't important to our markets as they change, we end up in a downdraft. That's why we have to identify the right Value Mix.

Value Mix	Core Value	Segment Value
Company	How general audiences perceive your company	How specific audience segments perceive your company
Product	The benefits broad audiences receive from your products	The benefits that each market segment receives from your product
Market	How you are perceived in your industry based on feedback and reputation	How you are perceived in specific markets based on supporters in that market and your word-of-mouth strength

Value Mix in Action

My client had been a health benefits administrator for midsize to large businesses for a number of years. (Note that this is a very simplified Value Mix. I don't want to give away the recipe for my client's secret sauce, so some values specifically have not been mentioned to protect their growth.) They offered a range of products and had a fabulous customer reputation. I met them as they were seeking opportunities to leverage their customer base for broader revenue opportunities. They also wanted to capture new customers with their wider array of services. But their first step was to determine their current Value Mix so they could create a strategy for evolving it.

As the team worked through the value segments and reached out to customers and supporters to get feedback, we found that a few key values resonated across all categories and markets: simple to work with, trusted experts, financial gains and great service. In fact, these values were so consistent we knew we needed to focus on and enhance those same core and segment values when selecting expansion opportunities.

Initial Value Mix

Value Mix	Core Value	Segment Value
Company	Simple health benefits	**Employer:** We do the work, you don't have to **Employee:** The company everyone trusts
Product	Financial savings	**Employer:** Significant financial savings & happy employees **Employee:** Simple way to save for my health costs
Market	The best service around	**Employer:** No more angry phone calls **Employee:** Someone to call for help

Based on their Value Mix and other factors (that we'll get into in later chapters), we determined that the up-and-coming focus on wellness was primed and waiting for their intrinsic values. We evolved their Value Mix to include specific values associated with wellness that they could deliver as distinct capabilities. We then created a strategic plan to enhance current offerings with more wellness-focused solutions: some an extension of current products, some the result of acquisitions or partnerships.

Evolved Value Mix

Value Mix	Core Value	Segment Value
Company	Simplifying your health	**Employer:** We do the work, you don't have to **Employee:** The company everyone trusts
Product	Personal and financial health	**Employer:** Significant savings, happy and healthy employees bring more productivity **Employee:** Simple savings, proactive health focus and a healthier me
Market	The best service around	**Employer:** No more angry phone calls, helping employees stay healthy **Employee:** Saving money, better health and it's easy

The changes are subtle—as they should be. We want a graceful evolution, not a disruptive Big Bang!

- We carried forward the key values of simplicity, expertise, financial savings and great service that were distinct in the minds of customers.

- We expanded our value delivery to include a broader range of products and focused on assuring wellness while managing health savings. We made sure that our new value was in sync with the same key health values from both an employer and an employee perspective. (In this case, segment values were based on the consumers of services, not different industries or segments.)

The result? We successfully increased revenues and margins, establishing a strong leadership position in an emerging—and rapid-growth—marketplace.

The goal of a Value Mix is to help you focus on a compelling and coordinated set of values that work in concert to fuel your growth. Less is always better when it comes to your value focus. The key is to get focused and stay focused on an attainable, well-defined Value Mix that represents your value for today and tomorrow. Once you have clearly defined that mix, you'll cross-reference it with your market opportunities to create a sustainable growth plan.

Growth comes when you evolve your Value Mix in sync with your market opportunities. Options for evolution are as diverse as your imagination. The only rule is that you stay in sync with your market opportunity and your core value—no left turns or reversals in course without thoughtful discussions. When you stay on course and evolve as you go, you can profitably grow.

PILOT HANDBOOK: THE DYNAMICS OF VALUE

1. **Defining value is the first step in planning for strategic growth.** Before we begin to evolve ourselves or expand our markets, we must understand the value that powered us to our current point in time.

2. **Sustainable value is rarely found in a single asset or product.** Value is a blend of tangible and intangible assets as perceived by our audiences.

3. **Identifying value is complex.** That's because what's powerful value to one customer is ho-hum to another. We must perceive our value through the eyes of our diverse audiences, integrating their perspectives into powerful, yet consistent, value threads.

4. **Your Value Mix represents the fuel that creates forward thrust for your business.** Included in your Value Mix are values for your:

   - **Company:** Our company value is more than a building or a brand, a product or a service. Our company value must remain true as we evolve our product offerings.

   - **Product:** Product value goes far beyond features. Product value comes from a key problem we solve for a customer, our deep expertise, simplicity of use or our attractive packaging—just to name a few examples.

   - **Market:** Market value is the most powerful of all values. Market value is based on our oomph, the power we enjoy in certain sectors based on evidence of our customers' success and on word-of-mouth credibility.

5. **There are two forms of value:**

   - **Core value** represents the essence of our business, the reason we came to be in the first place. Core value evolves much more slowly than segment value. Core value reflects our overall mission and often is the reason we came to be in business.

   - **Segment value** provides our turbo-boost in specific market or customer profiles. Segment value may vary from audience to audience. It evolves more quickly than core value. When we evolve segment value in sync with market changes, we power consistent growth.

   We blend core and segment values in unique ways to deliver compelling and distinct value for each of our target audiences.

The Bottom Line. Value powers us to business velocity. Yet value is a special blend of tangible and intangible aspects for every company. A strong Value Mix is the powerful fuel we need to reach for sustainable growth.

CHAPTER 10

Where's Your Value?

Value is in the eye of the beholder.

Everything we need to know about our future is in the eyes and hearts of our customers. They know their present needs and how we are supporting them today. They can offer advice for ways to improve and enhance our value. They also know their future: the progress they want to make, the challenges they expect to face. Their insights will guide our successful evolution—when we listen.

The distinction customers see as our value is often very different from what we believe to be true. That's a fact that must drive every value, opportunity and growth decision we make. If we haven't validated our decision with multiple and varied customers and prospects, then that decision is just an assumption. Usually it's an assumption based on our own status quo thinking, which makes it even more dangerous. Besides, we all know what happens when we assume, right?

How do you find your value? Let's look at the sources and find out!

Tangible and Intangible Values

Value is a complex equation.

We tend to view our value in terms of quantitative and tangible evidence, with measures that offer clear results (e.g., market share or revenue growth). But that's not how buyers see our value.

Buyers are driven by evidence, but they're also compelled by value that impacts them personally: for instance, that counter clerk who always remembers your name or the customer service rep who just will not give up on solving a problem. Qualitative and intangible value is often more power-ful than quantitative and tangible value.

You must identify these qualitative and intangible factors when you define your Value Mix. To miss these key motivators is to miss your most powerful fuel.

- Value can be as tangible as a brand that is renowned—look at Apple or Disney.
- Value can be as intangible as a waiter's welcoming smile and helpful nature, which bring us back again and again to that same restaurant.
- Value can be a key feature that our buyers need today or the ease of service and support we deliver tomorrow.

For example, why do we choose the hotels that we favor?

- Is it the price of the room, the location, the health club, the room ser-vice or the great pool that attracts us?
- Maybe it's that frequent traveler reward program that helps us afford our family vacations or weekend getaways.
- Or it's the front desk staff who not only remember us, but also put us in our favorite room with that superb sunset view.

That's why the right Value Mix is so important. The right value focus fuels our growth; the wrong assumptions about our value cause a stall. If the hotel decides to fire that helpful man-ager you've always relied on for those special perks, would you return? Maybe not. If they expand the health club when it's not some-thing that most of their customers use, will it help them grow? Doubtful.

> Asking "So What?" helps us identify compelling value through the eyes of our audiences.

Whether I'm working to create a new strategy or a new company posi-tion, I always ask myself one simple question to get anchored in the eyes of my customers—"So What?" So what does my customer receive as value? So what do they perceive as their results? So what will they think about my offering? Once I start thinking from that perspective, I begin to ask the keepers of the truth—my audience—about their perspectives. We'll go into more detail about your keepers later in the chapter. For now, let's take a deeper look at those three aspects of value we discussed at length in the previous chapter.

Your Company Value

The following table lists some real-world examples of company value based on target audience perceptions. Take a look at the core and segment values of these brand names and think about how you can find your company value.

Company Value Examples

Company	Core Value	Segment Value
Apple	Easy-to-use entertainment, communication and information	**Kids:** Owning Apple stuff is cool **Adults:** Anyone can use anything from Apple **Designers:** Apple offers great graphics expertise
Proctor and Gamble	Helping make our lives cleaner, brighter and easier	**Mothers:** I can trust P&G products **Dads:** Offers affordable products that help me do what I need to do for my family
Pampers	Making babyhood simpler	**New Mothers:** I can trust that my newborn is comfortable **Mothers:** The folks who make Pampers understand how babies grow **Dads:** Even I can change a baby
Betty Crocker	Delicious, simple-to-prepare meals	**Moms:** My family thinks I'm a good cook because of the foods and recipes **Dads:** Even I can make meals

Obviously, I've simplified these to make my point. Each core value reflects the theme of the company, forming the flexible yet stable boundaries for its value focus. Segment values play to specific market segments or audiences.

Emotions are often at the center of value. Your value is as much about how you impact the lives of your buyers as it is about your business results. That's why asking "So What?" is so important. To clearly identify value, you must understand how you help your buyer. Remember, even B2B companies are ultimately selling to a person.

Where's Your Company Value?

To find your value begin by speaking with your audiences. Later in this chapter we'll discuss how to select the best audience for your value discussions. At this point, let's focus on the best questions to determine your perceived values—both tangible and intangible. Here are some questions I always ask my audiences to get the ball rolling.

1. What comes into your mind when you hear our company name?

You're searching for customers' high-level perspectives on your core value. Get them to talk about how they perceive your company instead of features or product-specific details. When you gather multiple perspectives from diverse buyers, you'll find a thread of value that permeates your business. That's your core value.

For example, if someone asks me this question concerning AT&T, my answer would be "the oldest communications company in the business." Old in that case reflects experience and the value derived from that longevity. It also implies that AT&T has survived through all of the ups and downs in communication markets, which means they're likely to be around for the longer term—offering security and peace of mind. That's my perspective as their buyer.

2. What is the most valuable thing we offer you? Why?

The answer might be a product, a service, a person—virtually anything that the customer finds valuable. To gain useful insights, probe for information about all aspects of the company. These value points will help you confirm your core value and build your segment lists.

Asking "Why?" helps you get more information about the customer's specific application or use of your solutions. The answers to the "why" help you formulate your segment values for the specific audiences you're targeting. In chapter 12 I'll discuss how to take the input you collect and use it to strengthen your mapping between market opportunities and value.

3. Why did you buy from us?

Why do you keep buying from us? Again, steer away from product and feature discussions. I usually probe a bit to ask how the audience perceives a brand, a market image, all of the qualitative and intangible aspects of a company. Sometimes the same core thread flows throughout the entire conversation. That shows a stable value and consistent brand, which is great news. Just make sure that the stable value is applicable to your future markets.

On the other hand, static doesn't exist anymore, so a single value thread can also signal a waning value, if you're experiencing a downturn or declining wins. Probe a bit deeper to find out if that value is still distinct. You may be looking at a consistent value that needs to evolve.

When you hear one response for why customers made an initial purchase and a different response for why they keep buying from you, you've found an evolution or expansion path in your value. Pay attention to that path, especially when you're speaking with early-adopter audiences. You just found your expansion route for current customers and a path for your own value evolution.

4. How do you view our company versus other vendors in our market?

I know I said to leave the competition out of your growth planning, but this is one case where it's good to collect a perception of your competition. You won't use this to guide your future strategy. Rather, it will give you a better perspective on your own value and its position with respect to the competition. If no competitor is perceived to be comparable, you have a clear and unchallenged value. If others—even one competitor—are perceived to be similar, then you must focus on further differentiating your value from the alternative(s) to win.

5. What negative impressions can we address about our company for you?

You're right; this isn't looking for value. Now you're seeking areas that need to be addressed before you can expect to reach sustainable growth. Small issues like a bad customer-support call or a packaging problem are interesting but not cause for large strategic action. Larger issues—such as the perception of your company as uncaring, with dysfunctional support—are absolutely something you must address. It's always better to understand the potential negatives and plan for correcting them than to be blindsided when they crop up. So just ask!

Your Product Value

More than in any other area, we're best served when we define product value relative to our audience perspectives and not our own beliefs. We're simply too close to our products and services to have an objective viewpoint. We just don't see the world through our buyers' eyes, no matter how much time we spend with customers. That's why we need their direct input regarding product and service value.

What is a compelling product core value? Ask a simple "So What?" and you'll find out.

If you're in a B2B market, seek out hard evidence of the bottom-line impact your solutions brought your customers: cost reductions, increased profits, acceleration in productivity, competitive advantage. Then move to the more intangible and personal value your products provide: getting home on time from work, no more weekend crises, getting promoted or less stress on the job. If you're in a consumer market, focus on the improvements in people's personal lives that your products deliver: feeling more confident, spending more time with families, simplifying life in general. Then add any financial or other impacts to those intangibles.

The table on the opposite page shows sample product values associated with a variety of larger companies. Companies tend to naturally align product values with their core values in many markets. At least initially. Apple isn't going to start delivering easy-to-use vacuum cleaners, any more than Dyson is going to deliver the Ball for an iPhone.

Product Value Examples

Company	Core Product Value	Segment Product Value
Apple	Connect with friends, movies and music. It's easy!	**Kids:** Cool colors and choices; the iTunes store has everything in one place **Businesses:** Everyone can use an Apple without a lot of training; their support makes it easy
Dyson	Floors and carpets are cleaner, with less time and effort	**New Buyers:** It's easier than ever to clean anywhere **Traditional Moms:** Dyson vacuums are what my mom used
General Electric	Decrease our electric bills and help save the planet	**Kids:** We're saving energy and our planet **Parents:** GE offers affordable lights for every part of the house
Starbucks	Beverages and more, any way we want it	**Kids:** Cool drinks and a place to play video games on our laptops **Adults:** Great coffee, and wireless too **Businesses:** An easy and effective place to meet clients

Your best case is when your audiences overlap in their segment value. It's easier to evolve since you have a narrower value focus. Look at Starbucks. Their key segment value points are their great atmosphere and that convenient wireless—for business professionals and for kids too! That same value is enjoyed by all, even if it is in different ways.

When segment value varies from segment to segment or audience to audience, evolution becomes more complicated. Apple is a good case in point. Companies really don't care about the product colors or the iTunes store, while the kids really dig it! This means Apple has multiple segment values for multiple audiences, making value evolution a balancing act between available resources and financial returns.

Where's Your Product Value?

Here are some questions I ask to identify product values.

1. What key value do we provide to you with our products?

Avoid collecting a laundry list. You're looking for one overriding value for each audience segment. No matter how many options for value you discuss with your audience, there is usually one that is dominant. You need to understand what that value is. After you get your arms around that one key value, you can discuss other values your audience wants to share.

By focusing on one major benefit that permeates your audiences, you can prioritize and put boundaries around your product evolutions. Sometimes that top value is the result of multiple features. That's okay. Make sure you understand why that value is so important for your customers today, and then learn how to evolve it for tomorrow. Don't assume it's related to a specific feature or the innovation behind that feature. You'll end up downed by gravity as that feature becomes a drag, even as competitors deliver better value.

2. What other value would you like us to offer in our products or services?

Yep, that's a leading question. Exactly what you want. As long as you're talking with buyers about value, ask them about their next challenges, specifically the ones associated with how they use your products today. You can learn a lot from the vision of your audiences, especially the early adopters in emerging markets. The more closely you align your product evolution with their future needs, the better opportunity you have for growth.

3. What other important value do we provide with our products?

Now you begin to capture all areas of product value. I define one or two (with a max of three) segment values for each audience for strategic planning purposes. Often, feedback leads us to identify more than three values.

Parse the results as we discussed in chapter 9 so you have, preferably, one segment value. As with your core value, the best case is when your segment values are consistent across markets: that makes it a straightforward task to focus your evolution. When segment values differ widely across market and audience profiles, you have the task of prioritizing evolution based on revenues today and growth for tomorrow. We'll discuss how to handle that prioritization in the form of flight routes in chapter 13.

4. What can you accomplish now that you couldn't before you bought our products?

You need to understand how your value is applied in your customers' worlds. For some markets, it's relatively clear-cut. For example, *"That new eye shadow really makes my eyes stand out!"* In other markets, it's much more complex. For example, *"We couldn't have designed our new aircraft without the ability to process terabytes of information in our central site and then deliver that information to five thousand users around the globe."* One is a simple benefit; the other gets much more complicated. That isn't the point. The goal is to learn which benefits your product value brings to your customers' world. You'll later quantify these advantages in terms of market opportunity to help prioritize both your markets and your value evolution.

5. Please share a simple story of that value.

As long as you're asking, you may as well capture the details. You can use them later for customer success studies and anecdotes. Such customer stories deepen your understanding of your products' value. I also often find that stories from diverse customer segments overlap in some common area of value or way of using a product. Those overlaps represent leverage points to power your growth.

Customer case studies also come in handy for finding areas of product value. If you've developed those stories based on "So What?" benefits versus strict product capabilities, you're ahead of the game. The more product benefits and value you understand, the better you can triangulate your core and segment value points.

Once you've gathered your product value feedback, there's one more step before you blend your Value Mix. Indeed, it may be the most powerful of all values.

Your Market Value

Market value comes from success, not from Wall Street.

Market value is created through word-of-mouth credibility, combined with the evidence of our benefits (market share, customer power, revenue growth). Think about how you buy a new important whatever in your life, be it a car, a washing machine or a speedboat. Do you read what the company says about themselves and their products, or do you go talk to your friends and read the expert opinions about the product?

We seek out our peers or people who advise our peers, right? So if all the evidence pointed to one speedboat as the winner, but none of our friends liked it, we wouldn't necessarily buy that speedboat. If another had the best reputation among our friends, and the evidence said it was an okay choice, we'd decide to buy that boat. Sometimes we'll even buy what our friends recommend regardless of what the supposed experts say. That's the power of market value.

Sure, we can claim market value based on our market share or number of customers. We can have the best analyst report or *Consumer Reports* review. But if we have no customers willing to stand up and recommend us, we won't go very far. If we don't have supporters behind all those numbers, we won't have the numbers to flaunt much longer anyway.

> A satisfied customer is the best business strategy of all.
> —Michael Leboeuf

When we keep our growth strategies in line with our strongest market value, we further increase our power. I often use market value to fine-tune priorities for a growth strategy. If we have a choice between two otherwise equal markets to pursue, the market with the most powerful value and loudest ambassadors is probably the best choice. That extra thrust of market credibility can make the difference between struggling to take off and quickly reaching business velocity.

Here are some examples of companies with great market value.

Market Value Examples

Company	Core Market Value	Segment Market Value
IBM	70 years of leadership Recognized as the leader in business computing	**Executives:** Trust that IBM will solve their problems **Users:** Trust IBM as their source of great computing systems **Technical:** Know they won't lose their jobs for buying IBM
Crest	ADA recommended 70+ years of commitment to dental health	**Adults:** Our teeth have never been brighter **Moms:** I trust Crest with my children's teeth **Kids:** Crest tastes great and comes in my favorite flavor
Volvo	Known as the safest vehicle for our family	**Parents:** We trust Volvo to keep our kids safe, even in an accident **Teens:** Safe and fun, with cool new styling **Adventurers:** Safe and I can take it anywhere I want to go
Sears	Recognized for decades as the retailer you can trust	**Homeowners:** Price-competitive appliances, great service **Families:** Great clothing and accessories at prices we can afford

Where's Your Market Value?

Market power is created when we deliver on the promise of our company and product values.

Market value comes in all shapes and forms. To find your market value, look for both the tangible evidence and the intangible support that fuels your credibility.

EXAMPLES OF VALUE

Company Value

Tangible: Experience, longevity, recognized expertise, area of focus

Intangible: Trusted, great customer service, smiling faces, knowledgeable staff, brand

Product Value

Tangible: Fastest, most powerful, broadest selection, lowest cost, cool capability

Intangible: Easy, dependable, love my sales clerk, all my friends use it too

Market Value

Tangible: Number of customers, years in that market, firsts and innovation

Intangible: They saved my business; they understand my problems

Tangible evidence is easy to gather if you've created value in your markets. Examine all aspects, including the number of customers (and notable customers) in a specific market, first-evers or special things that you've accomplished in that market space, such as an innovation you've introduced. Longevity and success can also fuel market value. The goal is to find anything that evidences your commitment to, and value in, this specific segment. Sometimes segments are defined by industry, sometimes by customer size, sometimes by age groups or specific profiles. Segment your evidence to match the markets you address in whatever form makes sense to your business. Then go find the evidence that proves your power. Once you have that evidence, add your audience's support, and the next thing you know, you're flying high.

Intangible evidence appears in the form of stories and testimonials by customers and partners, industry leaders and other influencers. As part of your discussions with your keeper audiences, you'll naturally collect the intangible evidence of market power.

Once your market power is identified, the next step is to bring the tangible and intangible into alignment. That alignment shows where you have deep (or shallow) market power. You can then apply that value (or lack thereof) when creating your growth strategy.

We've reviewed the various sources of value. We've also offered some questions to ask your audience and yourselves to identify your most powerful value aspects. Now let's take a look at the audience members who will provide the truth about your value.

The Keepers of the Truth

Trusted market feedback fuels our business growth. Following the wrong advice throttles our growth.

Selecting the best sources of input is just as important as asking the right questions. Not every customer today is a great future customer. Nor is every winning market today likely to be an opportunity for high growth tomorrow. We need a blend of input, balanced proportionately across our past, our present and our future.

How do you profile the best audience for feedback? I select some of each, depending on the situation at hand. Here are the sources of feedback I include.

Big customers in our major markets. Even with the risk of gravity they bring, their input is important. Blend it with input from newer and emerging market customers to get a balanced perspective, giving it only the weight it deserves. Don't pick your favorite customers. Find new major sources of revenue and listen. Then go back and chat with that favorite customer to see how closely aligned they are with other buyers. That gives you a quick check on your course. If your biggest customer's feedback is out of sync with that of other growth markets, you need to evolve, restricting the impact this customer has on your overall direction. Following their perceptions will only negatively impact your future growth.

Smaller customers from a diversity of growing markets. Identify the markets that are growing and gather feedback. Pick the customers that are early adopters; they'll be the ones that lead the rest of that market forward. I had a customer once who focused on the leading accounts in one main sector, while giving minimal attention to a few other well-defined complementary markets. They'd entered these secondary markets to protect against being a one-market wonder, but really weren't spending much effort outside of their main sector. When we interviewed their smaller customers, we found one secondary market where my client had a highly distinct solution. No one else had come close to resolving these customers' issues. We realigned their prioritization and went full force into this marketplace, resulting in rapid market entry. They were the new leader in this space within twelve months, with this new secondary market providing larger gross profits than the larger legacy segment.

New customers in new markets. Pay attention to that handful of new customers coming on board, the ones with the new and different applications of your product. Their new and different could well become your future opportunity. Just look at Amazon. They started with a single focus on books. They listened to their customers, and as Amazon grew, they added new products and entered new markets—always being sure that they had interest from their customer base before they added new offerings. Today, you can buy almost anything you want on Amazon. Their growth demonstrates the success you can attain when you evolve and expand in sync with growing new markets.

Pipeline prospects. Prospects offer perspectives on your weakness as well as your strength. By identifying and addressing weakness in your business, you can create additional value and fine-tune your targets. For example, I once had a client who suddenly began losing all new business opportunities in a specific market. We asked prospects from that market about my client's value and learned that a competitor had integrated a number of small products into their offering, simplifying everyone's life. No wonder they were winning. My client had two choices: abandon the market or evolve. They chose to evolve, integrating an even better product offering from a larger vendor in that space. They killed two birds with one stone: they quickly filled their value gap and they leveraged a well-respected vendor to power their own leadership in that space.

Suspects. We all have gut intuition about a new market, an emerging opportunity and the next set of changing winds that are going to hit our business. Don't wait for these suspects to appear; seek them out in prospective buyers, partners and industry thought leaders. Identifying that next big growth front is your chance to lead. Remember, it's always easier to capture a market early in its growth, before competitors step in and take the lead.

Naysayers. Sometimes you gather your best feedback from those who don't exactly like you. I always find a few curmudgeons to chat with about my clients: a lost account, the guys who drive their customer service reps nuts. Listening to their perspectives helps you find holes, learn which areas need improvement and expand your reality. Be selective about which naysayers you include. My ideal targets are the buyers who represent that customer profile you want to win—but where you've been unsuccessful to date. It doesn't take a long chat with a naysayer to determine whether the dissatisfaction was related to a specific situation, a personal vendetta or was because you simply can't compete in that market. You may be able to evolve and win. Find out for sure!

There are also broader members of your audience who can give you great feedback beyond a customer's perspective. Some other keepers include:

Partners. Partners are one of the best sources of objective feedback (well, mostly objective). They hear things from customers and see your employees in action in the real world. Whenever I'm working with a client on a strategy, partners are one of the first places I look for objective feedback.

Partners come in a number of different flavors.

Product partners help develop solutions or offer complementary products that make both our products more valuable. For example, all the suppliers of iPhone gaming applications are product partners for Apple.

Distribution partners resell your products, add services around those products and help your customers buy and use your offerings. Wal-Mart, for example, is a distribution partner for many of its suppliers.

Then there are the partners who coexist in your customers' world. They may not directly engage with your products and services, but you end up working together in some aspects to make your customers happy.

Any and all types of partners offer invaluable insights into gravity, value and markets. Take that product partner who has a strong customer base in that juicy market segment you're dying to own. There's a strong source of feedback for future opportunities and the value you must deliver to win. That distribution partner who interacts with your customers on a daily basis is also a significant source of feedback. Make sure the partners you seek are trusted to be objective—then listen and learn.

Industry experts. Often, we don't like what these folks may have to say: the analyst who believes that your competitor's approach is the only way to solve a problem; the known leading-edge end user who has an ingrained passion for another competitor; the critic who didn't like the consistency of your chili compared to the chili in the restaurant his nephew owns. That's just the way it goes. For all the industry experts who are in some vendor's hip pocket, there are also objective folks who act as experts in your markets. Those are the experts you want to listen to and follow.

Sure, you lose some business because of biased industry experts, but you can offset those losses by cultivating and listening to their objective brethren. Plus, end-user buyers are pretty smart about discounting those experts who are always stomping for one particular vendor.

Focus on the experts who are bright, independent thinkers. Listen to their feedback, learn from them and then take their suggestions to heart. Include their suggestions in your evolutionary path. When they see their ideas at play in your strategies, you will also win them over as one of your market ambassadors.

Along with these external resources, your employees can likewise be keepers of the truth—if you listen with an objective ear. I said earlier that what we think doesn't really matter, so the idea of polling internal resources might confuse you. I'm not suggesting you ask your employees about your values and strategies. I am suggesting you ask the right employees about what they hear from your customers. Sure, some of their personal opinions may skew their perceptions, but you can still learn some pretty interesting things. Especially when it comes to holes in your value or those supposedly ideal markets your sales reps are pushing that aren't such a great fit after all. Customer anecdotes shared with your teams provide valuable input for your growth path.

Here are the places I look internally for additional feedback.

Sales. I don't mean the biggest sales reps in traditional markets. Don't even go there. Talk to the reps who are selling in new spaces, in emerging markets, for new applications or to new customer profiles. These are the representatives who are breaking new ground, who are thinking out of the status quo box and into a new future. What they learn gives you priceless insight into your next best market opportunities. Those legacy sales reps can sometimes be a source of gravity, so keep a watchful eye on their behaviors and be thoughtful about their input. Keep your gravity in check!

Field service. If you want to find out the truth about your products, talk to the field representatives who support them on a constant basis. Too often we lump the field support personnel in with the sales group. Their interactions with customers may well be different. Chat with the people who sell your products at the department stores, the traveling representatives who maintain a customer base with quarterly visits. They have first-hand input about customer reactions and comments—the good, the bad, and the ugly. Seek out those stories, both positive and negative. That's fair fodder for value discussion, and it's even more critical when you begin planning your flight.

Customer service. One of the most overlooked keepers of the truth is your own customer service department. These folks chat with your customers every day. They can tell you the truth about what's really working and what's not. Just remember that service reps are communicating mainly with customers who have problems, so expect your staff to have more stories with a negative focus. Be prepared and balance your responses accordingly.

Pick and choose from these categories to define the best audience for input—based on the information you're seeking. For example, if I'm researching product value, I'll include pretty much all of the categories presented. If I'm looking for company value, I'll focus more on current customers and industry experts. For market value, I'll look to customers of all types, as well as partners and my sales representatives. They'll often point me to more potential sources of feedback. By the way, each keeper is also a potential source of market value and support. Recruit them while you're at it!

As with all things, gathering feedback and input is a dynamic exercise. A great source today may not be the best source tomorrow. When we identify the best combination of sources, we'll find the truth we seek by listening with an objective mind.

 ## Which Truth Is Your Truth? A Value Mix in Action

BizTech supplied specialized computing solutions to small-to-midsize businesses, helping them automate back office processes for improved efficiency. The company was preparing to launch its next great product innovation: a new suite of computing solutions designed to process even more data, faster and more efficiently than ever before. The technology was leading-edge; the company was excited as could be; and a huge launch was in the budget to assure that the company made its mark with this new offering.

The table at the bottom of the page shows their initial Value Mix.

Now the task was to evolve or validate this baseline to create the best Value Mix possible for BizTech. The first thing we did was chat with a number of their current customers and partners to validate the company's value today. We also presented the new products to this same audience to get their reaction. Then we took the suite of new products to some enterprise buyers who represented the new target segment for BizTech's latest innovations. Some of the reactions we heard are shown in the table on the opposite page.

BizTech Initial Value Mix

Value Mix	Core Value	Segment Value
Company	The leader in scalable computing	**Enterprise:** Proven value, revolutionary innovation **SMB:** The company who cares
Product	Computing the way YOU want it	**Enterprise:** Scalable, fast, proven computing solutions **SMB:** Faster, flexible computing
Market	We focus on your business	**Enterprise:** We can solve any problem **SMB:** Proven SMB expertise

BizTech Audience Input

Current Value, Current Customers	New Product, Current Customers	New Product, Target Customers
"BizTech understands my business better than any vendor out there. They help me match a system to make sure my business runs smoothly." (CEO, mid-size business—$250M in revenue)	"If BizTech thinks that system can work for me, I'll try it. But I'm just not sure why I need to change. What I have works. Why complicate things?" (CEO, midsize business—$250M in revenue)	"Who's BizTech? I've never heard of them. I don't work with start-ups—too much hassle." (CIO, Fortune 1000 corporation)
"BizTech products just keep working. I don't have to worry about a big IT staff or specialists to keep them running efficiently. Anyone can do it." (Owner, small business—$50M in revenue)	"I don't think so. It looks complicated, and I'll have to hire an IT person. I don't have the budget to do that, especially since my system works today." (Owner, small business—$50M in revenue)	"These systems look like just the thing I need. But I'll need proof that they work. Are there reference customers in my industry with similar complexity?" (CIO, large financial institution)
"I'm just another small business to all the other enterprise vendors. BizTech is focused on SMB—they think I'm important. I know they'll be there for me." (VP, IT, midsize business—$100M in revenue)	"That looks like an enterprise system to me. I hope BizTech isn't going to abandon me to go play with the big boys. I need their service and support." (Systems Manager, midsize business—$100M in revenue)	"The value is obvious—I just don't know that I trust the company. What other large clients do they have? Can I chat with other large customers?" (CIO, large healthcare services firm)
"I don't need the latest technology. I want what works. That's why I use BizTech. Their systems do what I need, without complications." (COO, mid-size business—$150M in revenue)	"I can see some advantages to larger-scale system as I grow. I just don't want to lose today's simplicity. If that's the case, I won't switch." (COO, midsize financial systems—$150M in revenue)	"I think this is a great innovation, but I'm already working with IBM and I don't see a reason to change." (COO, consumer products division of Fortune 100 corporation)
"I know that whenever I have a problem, BizTech will be there to help me solve it. They are like my own IT staff whenever I need them." (CEO, small business—$40M in revenue)	"Wow, that looks kinda complicated. I really don't need all those bells and whistles, I'm fine with what I have." (CEO, small business—$40M in revenue)	"I'd be willing to try it. But I'll need a full support team on-site—say 5 people full time. My current vendor has that many people dedicated to me. Biztech needs to match that." (CIO, midsize enterprise services)

What We Learned

Obviously, this is a simplified version of a value exercise. But there's enough input to see some common threads of value, as well as some issues with the current plan.

1. Small and medium-size business customers love BizTech. Why? They focus on SMB, they have experience in SMB and they show up to support their SMB customers.

2. SMB customers love BizTech's current product value, which is that it *just works*. They aren't seeking more bells and whistles; they like simple.

3. BizTech saves SMBs a lot of money and time because they don't need a big IT staff to manage their systems.

4. SMB customers don't want BizTech to focus more broadly. Current customers worry that they'll lose that personal touch as BizTech focuses on large accounts.

5. Enterprise vendors don't know BizTech. They like the new technology value but want proof in the form of customer references from within their own industries. That means BizTech has a lot of market creation to do.

Given these observations, we concentrated on the SMB customer base for our Value Mix. It was obvious we needed to take a more in-depth look at the enterprise opportunity before we determined an attack plan. The company's former claims about its new product value in both the enterprise and the SMB markets were unstable and a bit off target: enterprise buyers didn't view the company as a serious player, and BizTech's current SMB markets didn't view all of the new product's value as necessary. Launching that product into the market based on the initial mix was not a smart strategy. We risked losing the confidence of current SMB customers as we appeared to abandon them for the bright lights of the enterprise market.

What We Did About It

We focused on winning value for the company and its products—specific value that could be demonstrated and supported by compelling customer statements in markets that were available to BizTech. Here's the evolved Value Mix we defined.

BizTech Evolved Value Mix

Value Mix	Core Value	Segment Value
Company	Simple Business Computing	We help make SMBs successful
Product	It just works!	Simple computing saves money Designed to keep your business going
Market	We help make SMBs successful	We understand SMB We save SMBs money We help SMBs grow

- We defined the value in terms that the SMB audience used, eliminating the upscale technical jargon focused on the enterprise buyer.

- As you'll see, every value links to every other value in the mix. Company value establishes that BizTech is indeed a leader in simple business computing, with the credentials to prove it. This value positions BizTech as an expert in the SMB market, which then sets up the firm's product and market values.

- Product value shows why BizTech is a leader: their products are simple, they work and they save their customers money. That's what SMB wants, not all the innovative leading-edge features and cool stuff that enterprise businesses often seek.

- Market value lets BizTech's best promoters tell their story, which is that BizTech helps your SMB business be successful, saving money and increasing efficiency thanks to simple computing systems.

We realigned the Value Mix to reflect reality today, while understanding the value that could come for tomorrow. We weren't saying we would never pursue the enterprise market, just that we didn't have the required value to enter the market at this time.

———————

Once you've defined your value—especially your core value—stick to it. Use that value to guide your evolution for growth. But value isn't value unless it has a market. The next steps are to map your value to market opportunities and then create a strategic plan to reach for the incremental growth available in multiple opportunity markets.

PILOT HANDBOOK: WHERE IS YOUR VALUE?

1. **Value is in the eyes of the beholder.** Our audiences keep the truth about our value. What we think about any of our values really doesn't matter; what matters is how our audience perceives us.

2. **Value is a complex equation.** It includes both evidence and purely emotional responses. Value comes in both tangible and intangible forms. A blend of interdependent and very dynamic experiences and beliefs determines buyer preferences, which determine value.

3. **Asking "So What?" is the best way to dive deeply into audiences' perceptions of our value.** So what value does my company bring? So what value does my product bring? So what difference do I make in the lives of my customers?

4. **Company value is more than a building or a brand, a product or a service.** Company value comes from a blend of tangibles and intangibles. Never underestimate the power of the intangible when collecting company value. Questions to pinpoint company value include:
   - What comes into your mind when you hear our company name?
   - What is the most valuable thing we offer to you? Why?
   - Why did you buy from us? Why do you keep buying from us?
   - How do you view our company versus other vendors in our market?
   - What negative impressions can we address about our company?

5. **Product value goes far beyond features.** Product value focuses on the differences our solutions make, or the problems they solve, in our customers' businesses, careers or everyday lives. The "So What?" question helps determine product value. Specific questions to ask to pinpoint product value include:
   - What key value do we provide to you with our products?
   - What other important values do we provide with our products?
   - What can you accomplish that you couldn't before you bought our product?
   - Share a simple story of that value.
   - Why else did you choose our product?

6. **Market value comes from success.** The measure of market value is the power of our support in that market. For every customer or partner success, we attain more fuel than just revenue; we capture recommendations. Word-of-mouth support is the strongest value we can have, in any market.

The Bottom Line. Value isn't a single line item on a check sheet. It's a complex and extremely dynamic attribute of your business. When you recognize your true value, you create compelling growth momentum. When you make poor assumptions about your value, you limit your business growth.

CHAPTER 11

Horizons of Opportunity

Opportunity is all around us. That's why we need to focus.

To soar, we must stay in sync with our markets—understanding where our value resonates well; sensing when that resonance begins to fade; searching for our next opportunity and the next one after that. Initial growth comes from focusing on specific markets that have a strong demand for our value. Sustainable growth comes from dynamically adjusting our focus—in terms of our value and our opportunities—as the marketscape around us evolves.

Our market horizons continuously change, driven by any number of dynamic events: the inherent behaviors of business buyers; the competitive alternatives that appear when we least expect it; and economic pressures that can ground us for good—just to name a few.

Markets represent horizons of opportunity. As we head toward any point on that horizon, we may find updrafts and downdrafts, sheer or big business lift. We must continuously watch our horizon for signs of change, realigning ourselves to take best advantage of our current course and targets today, while simultaneously planning an intercept course with emerging market opportunities for tomorrow. Opportunity Horizons empower us to do just that.

Opportunity Horizons

Think of your market horizon as a series of contiguous points, each representing a different market segment. Every point is moving on its own course, at its own speed and trajectory. Markets may be riding a wave or trend in the broader business environment or following their own trajectory based on their own size and gravity. Yes, your markets are subject to gravity as well. Each point is coming closer to, or moving away from, your current course, just as you can turn toward or away from those same market segments.

The first step when creating your own Opportunity Horizon is to segment your market as shown in the figure below. There are five categories I focus on during a market opportunity discussion with clients. These categories are current markets, complementary markets, emerging markets, left and right field markets and 20/20 markets.

As we explore the characteristics of each of the market categories in the next pages, think about your own trajectory and market focus. Identify where your target markets fall on your horizon today. Are they current market opportunities? Are they complementary? Or are you only pursuing emerging market opportunities? Each type of market segment comes with different

Opportunity Horizon

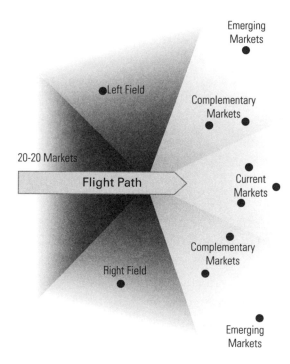

risks and rewards. Understanding how to best leverage each market segment helps you find the combination of market lift that you need to grow.

As you define your own horizon, don't make the assumption that one category holds a better or worse opportunity than another. Don't assume that the markets you are currently targeting are those that you should be targeting. As business history has shown us, you could very well be misled by those assumptions. Everything is situational; the best matches between market opportunities and your growth path depend on your Value Mix, current course and unique business situation.

Where's the Lift?

Lift comes in many forms. So do market opportunities. Sometimes a market takes a quick updraft; look at smartphones, for instance. Then there's a slow-building opportunity that suddenly explodes; think of the hybrid automobile. Opportunities are all around us. Your job is to pick the right ones to power growth for today, as you also watch for new opportunities to come closer into alignment with—or farther away from—your value and focus. Only by thoughtfully realigning your course and value as your markets evolve can you reach for sustainable growth.

Let's look at each of the five market categories in detail, including the rewards and risks each brings and how to use each to your best advantage.

Current Markets

Current markets are the easiest opportunities to identify, or at least they should be. I'm not asking for the markets you think you are pursuing—that is, the combination of your past successes and your wish list. Focus on the markets where you are profitably selling today in some volume, not just the one-offs.

So, how do you identify the truth about your current markets? Gather the numbers and parse them based on bottom-line results, versus the top-line revenue measures that many businesses tend to use. Let's say you learn that your biggest segment is driving a really low profit margin while that smaller emerging segment delivers four times the profit and is growing rapidly. Which one would you want to focus on for growth?

Be sure to go beyond the numbers. Ask the people who know the truth about your best market opportunities: the customer sales and service force. Don't be surprised if the sales reps are selling to a subset of what you believe are current market opportunities. Reps sell where they win; so, wherever they are winning, that's your current market focus. You'll find that your best sales reps do not waste time on the target markets you choose for them. Great reps expend their efforts where they can win. If they can't make big dollars, they move on. Where they focus is your current market opportunity, whether you want to believe it or not. Pay attention.

I'm not saying that you should let your sales force drive your growth strategy. I'm saying that you have to listen to your sales force because they may be more in tune with your best current market opportunities. Just be sure to ask the right folks in your sales force, not only the ones who may be stuck in gravity in those biggest customers. Chat with some who are focused on capturing new accounts. That's where the rubber meets the road when it comes to market opportunity matching your value in today's world.

But what about those other great target markets you know are ripe for your value? Why aren't your sales reps approaching them? Take a hard look at your value, mapping it to the demand in those targets. Something is missing to make you a winner. For example:

- If the market opportunity is more limited than you thought, or the market is unavailable thanks to a strongly entrenched competitor, or if your value is actually a poor fit, you need to move on to other markets. You just found another bit of status quo thinking that it's time to ditch.

- If there is an opportunity, but your value is slightly out of sync, make an informed thoughtful decision before you begin tuning value. Weigh the costs of enhancing value for this opportunity versus the opportunity present in other market segments. Businesses have limited resources so choose your spots for evolution wisely and with a full view of your Opportunity Horizon.

Current markets can deliver profitable growth for a long time to come, or they can be sliding as we speak. We'll get to the evaluation a bit later. For now, define the current markets that you're successful in today, including every segment from your largest revenue producers to your up-and-coming potential stars. Verify that you're really successful in these markets, and don't rely on wishful thinking.

Complementary Markets

Complementary markets offer the lowest-risk opportunities for business growth since they are associated in some way with your current targets. Usually they require minimal investment, smaller changes and less disruption than other alternatives. That can create a tailwind toward growth.

Customers in complementary markets display similar value requirements as those in current markets. For example, if you're already offering services to small businesses, expanding to include small office/home office opportunities might be a solid complementary expansion opportunity. You can package a subset of value, tuned to the SOHO needs, and efficiently grow. On the other hand, expanding to target enterprise accounts is probably not a wise growth strategy, since enterprises have such dramatically different needs than small businesses. The enterprise would represent a left or right turn in this case.

Complementary markets are especially important to consider when you've maxed the opportunity for profit in current markets. When current markets begin to commoditize or decline, adjusting course to include a complementary segment can help you fuel growth in new, yet familiar markets.

My favorite complementary markets are follower markets—the early majority adopter segments—because they can provide such a profitable growth opportunity. When you're already successful in an early adopter market segment, you can capture these following markets with minimal investment. You may need to fine-tune offerings or distribute through a new channel to meet their specific needs. But that's an easier investment than opening a distinctly different market—and less distracting to boot. Just be sure those following markets aren't already commoditizing to eliminate your profit. If that's happening, you may be better off seeking more profitable opportunities for growth, avoiding the gravity these specific following markets will bring.

You can also offer products that are complementary to your current offerings to foster growth. For example, if I'm carrying men and women's sportswear I might as well carry kids' wear too. The parents who buy for themselves also buy for their kids—and vice versa. I can grow revenues with minimal extra expense while covering overhead more easily thanks to a broader market audience.

Emerging Markets

Emerging markets power breakout velocity, enabling you to catch that big lift. They also carry big risk. Emerging markets are the least predictable of all. A strong updraft can appear out of nowhere, accelerate your growth and then fade to stillness, leaving you wondering what happened. At other times the strength builds over time, giving you the chance you need to align with and successfully capture that segment.

You must be your most dynamic to successfully fly in emerging markets: they can spin on a dime, dip and turn, climb and then stall. Sometimes it takes time for them to settle into a steady flow; sometimes it happens almost overnight.

Emerging markets can appear anywhere on the horizon. They may spin in from left field, pop up in association with a complementary market or even emerge right in the middle of your current course. Those are the bluebirds we all love to see fly across our path!

The closer an emerging market is to your current course, the easier it is to address it. Ideally you want to pursue only emerging markets that are relatively close to your current trajectory. But sometimes an opportunity is so compelling it's worth a change in course for your business.

For example, if your current space is commoditizing and all complementary markets are declining as well, emerging markets may be your best alternative. As your market value begins to decline, your margins will decline as well. More players enter and new innovation is introduced. Over time, value is commoditized. There's just not enough margin left to fuel your growth. Even new value can't create the margins you need to fuel growth in that overly mature market that you've enjoyed for the past years.

That's when emerging markets can fuel the next leg of your flight. You can test the waters and grow your presence in that market while leveraging your current market as the cash cow to hopefully cover your overhead as you adjust your course. As that emerging market grows, you can devote more resources to it, gradually shifting course from the lagging market toward this new uplift. Manage the transition in a way that best balances maintaining your cash flow from your legacy market with opening new opportunities for growth.

Status quo beliefs say that you have to invest heavily in an emerging market, not expecting profitability in the near term. After all, it takes these markets time to grow. That's no longer the case. An emerging market can reach escape velocity overnight. The best case is when we catch an emerging market as it begins its growth, quickly riding the updraft to profitable market leadership ahead of the competition.

Left and Right Field Markets

Left and right field markets offer breakout growth opportunities. They can also send you reeling. They require significant shifts in course, business model, offerings and often your business itself. Sometimes you need to make that turn due to your own circumstances. But that turn can also cause you to destabilize and fall. Be thoughtful.

Left and right field markets require different value and expertise than your current markets. For example, if I'm selling big diesel trucks to transportation companies, deciding to sell buses is a left turn. The customers are different, the service and support are different and the market requirements are different. The only thing they have in common is that the product is some form of transportation. I may take that left turn, especially if I'm losing money on the big diesel trucks. But to do so requires significant changes in my business. I must be thoughtful, examining all my options before I jump into any market just because it looks like a better path.

After we identify emerging market opportunities, we need to gather input in the form of market data and requirements. This can be challenging.

Our usual reaction is to apply the things we know about our current market to this very different market, which brings on status quo thinking and gravity. We need to objectively evaluate these markets, find their lift and their downdrafts and then apply our core value in the best manner for the markets' unique requirements.

Once you understand the needs of these markets, map them to your current business values. That mapping gives you the first analysis of each opportunity and what you need to do to create thrust in each market. Sometimes you'll see a sudden turn that could rip you apart, no matter how juicy the opportunity. At other times you'll find a real opportunity that is within your reach, just when you need a lift. Whether you decide to pursue these markets depends on your business situation. For example:

- Let's say you're a growing business with significant untapped potential in your current and complementary markets. The only reason to take any turn is if you can leverage your same core value into an even larger and still emerging opportunity.
- On the other hand, what if you're in a downward spiral caused by the collapse of your current and complementary markets (think about the financial and private lending industry in recent history)? You might jump right into that left field market as a course correction away from sure disaster. That assumes you can leverage your core and segment values in this segment.
- If you're in a turnaround mode and restarting your business from scratch—or in an early stage start-up just entering the market—you'd review your full range of opportunities before you decided to make a specific left or right turn.

If you decide to pursue a left field market, plot a course to intercept these markets with minimal disruption to your current business operations. In my experience, the best approach is to create a separate team for your initial efforts in this space. Empower a single team to focus on the emerging market's requirements, while isolating your mainline teams from distraction. Once you know that you can successfully capture these opportunities, you can reintegrate the team into your core business operations, creating a comprehensive plan to approach all of your markets in a leveraged fashion.

Taking a sudden sharp turn is not usually the best course of action—in business or in life. It's better to maintain stability by taking a series of gentler course corrections versus one Big Bang adjustment. Remember, evolution doesn't have to be the Big Bang. In fact, businesses are more successful when changes are continuous and less disruptive in nature.

20/20 Markets

Sometimes, you rediscover opportunities after the fact, markets that may have been interesting at some point in the past, but you've traveled forward on a slightly different course. It's natural to want to pursue these opportunities when they grow or become popular—or when you become desperate. After all, hindsight is 20/20.

Let's say you passed on a market last year because it just didn't look like a winner. The next thing you know, that same opportunity is growing like a rocket. It's tempting to return, isn't it? It's only been a year, you say to yourself. You can still get in there and win. Maybe you can, but more likely you can't. It depends on which other vendors have entered that market, how much market power they possess, how much impact a dramatic change in course will have on your current business trajectory and what you have to forgo to make that change.

Banking hard to chase 20/20 opportunities is usually not the optimum course for growth. Yet sometimes, it may be your best option. Once again, it's a situational decision.

- If that market's growing, there are bound to be leaders who already have velocity going for them. Why make a significant turn to take on a bigger competitor who is well entrenched?

- But what if you're already grounded due to government regulations or an unexpected market disaster? That 20/20 market may be a perfect fit for the value that remains in your business. In this situation, that 20/20 market may be just what you need to relaunch your business.

It all depends on your value, other available options and which course delivers the best momentum and opportunity to begin a new flight.

An abrupt and major change in course is rarely the best choice for a stable business. You can learn from these markets. If that 20/20 market is a true opportunity then the markets around it, both complementary and emerging, are likely opportunities for you. Evaluate these market segments and watch them closely. When you see a potential winner that's coming into alignment with your value further ahead, you can plot an intercept course—at a point in time that is optimal for your business growth.

MARKET CATEGORIES

Current markets—Where we actually sell today. Improving value and focus can bring immediate growth returns in these markets, especially with later adopters.

Complementary markets—Usually our best opportunities for expansion because they require minimal evolution, investment and distraction.

Emerging markets—A great source of future growth but also high risk. They can come from any point on your horizon. The key is early identification and planning to capture market share ahead of competitors.

Left and right field markets—Require thoughtful planning prior to any course correction. Depending on the situation, these can be opportunities for growth or demise.

20/20 markets—Be careful of 20/20 opportunities. We've moved beyond these, so they are best left where they are except in very specific situations.

Moving Targets

Your Opportunity Horizon is dynamic.

No point on the Opportunity Horizon will be in the same relative position one year, one month or perhaps even one week from now. A market that wasn't in our field of focus a few months ago may be directly in front of us

Evolving Opportunity Horizon

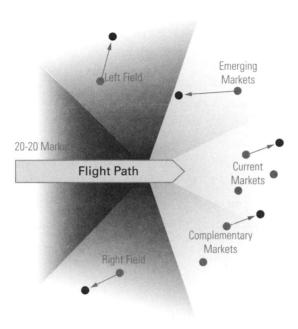

today. An emerging market we glossed over last year is now a high growth opportunity that will complement our course in the next few months. Our biggest market opportunity a year ago may be plummeting, leaving us searching for a new and profitable destination.

Competitors and partners are evolving as well. New competitors intersect our course as older ones fade away—or become stronger. Powerful partners fall behind as new ones emerge on our horizon.

To thrive in this ever-changing horizon, we must dynamically adjust our course, selecting our best route toward current and future opportunities to maintain growth.

- If your current market takes a nosedive, be ready to shift course toward a closely aligned market. You may even need to take a left turn.

- When you see a stronger tailwind in a complementary market, you may decide to adjust your course to take advantage of that acceleration for market expansion.

- That emerging market you've been watching may be just what you need to create sustainable growth two years from now. If you begin to evolve now you'll be more successful than if you wait until the opportunity is closer to you—and to your competitors.

The key is to be aware of your course and your entire horizon. With that awareness, you can subtly evolve both your value and your market focus as you move forward. Defining your market opportunities cannot be done in a vacuum. You must align your value with your opportunities to create a strategic map for your growth. I'll discuss how to align value with markets in the next chapter.

The key is focus. You can't try to capture every potential market opportunity; less is more. You must focus on the best opportunities, rather than spreading yourself so broadly that you never reach your ultimate destination—sustainable growth.

Opportunity Everywhere!

It often seems obvious which markets offer the best opportunities. But that's part of the challenge. We think it's obvious because we're stuck in our status quo beliefs. That keeps us rumbling along in pursuit of our known and comfortable markets. Either that, or it sends us spinning off into a whole new direction, making that big left turn when we suddenly look up and see our current course is a dead end. That's not the way to reach sustainable, continuous growth.

When working with clients to map key market opportunities, I always start defining the horizon with a brainstorming session. The goal is to capture all of the potential opportunities in this first phase. Don't be in a hurry to choose a course and destination. I don't recommend clients act on any of these markets—this is strictly brainstorming. Action will come later, as you'll see in chapters 12 and 13.

Be sure to involve folks from outside your core brain trust, including a range of customers.

- Bring in a few sales reps who are working with new markets or new applications of your current value. They are already thinking outside of your current focus.

- Bring in partners as well: the ones who are dabbling in left and right fields as well as in emerging spaces bring a fresh perspective.

- If you have business associates who are industry thought leaders, bring them in. But be careful. If they're viewed as the know-all experts, they can end up driving the brainstorming, with everyone following their lead. That brings a different form of gravity. A herd mentality is not a good approach to brainstorming!

How do you stimulate the brainstorming team to go beyond what you already know and believe? Think way outside the box and do things differently. I noted some ideas in chapter 1, including playing Stump the Chump and Shuffle the Deck. Here are a few more ideas specific to market opportunity brainstorming.

Start with a big blank whiteboard. Don't jump right in with your obvious choices of destination. That gets you stuck in the status quo before you have a flight plan. Start with a clean slate. Add the more obtuse opportunities first: rearview, left and right fields and emerging spaces. Spend time really thinking out of the corporate box: the wilder the better. Why wild? Because that gets you thinking differently from your status quo. And that's the first step to take as you defy gravity.

Stay outside the box. Before you get to the obvious current and complementary markets, spend some time evaluating the more abstract opportunities. Look for new derivative markets that may come closer to your current or a complementary course. Stay focused in your lesser-known markets and continue to brainstorm. Those spaces are where you often find the next generation of fuel for business growth.

Add the obvious. Layer in the current and complementary markets that are more obvious. Then check to see where these markets are relative to those newer markets you've already identified. Spend thoughtful time here. Identify strong value areas in your current markets that are comparable to the needs found in newer market opportunities. That gives you the chance to take test flights into those new markets with minimal evolution. Test flights help you gather the expertise and credibility you need to accelerate growth. These test flights can also create early momentum for your next flight. We'll discuss more about test flights in chapter 13.

Now you have a list of suspect opportunities. But you're not done. Markets are dynamic, so your list must be ever changing as well. Make it a point to check that list, adding new opportunities as they appear from all directions on your horizon. Adjust the position of markets already on your radar as their market velocity changes. Adjusting your list doesn't mean adjusting course toward these opportunities. It does mean keeping all market dynamics on your radar so you can make the necessary adjustments throughout your flight. Let's take a quick look at SC Johnson as an example.

Delivering Evolutionary Value— SC Johnson

I can still remember when we first used those flimsy Ziploc plastic bags to store our leftovers at home. They were a lot less expensive and easier to use than the bulky Tupperware containers, and we didn't have to wash them! We just tossed them away. So easy! Ziploc enhanced that product through the years: the bags became stronger and freezer ready, and the closure mechanism was supercharged. Then global warming became a big consideration in our lives. We all began to see the impact our plastic addiction had on planet Earth. Suddenly those bags didn't look so great anymore, at least not in my house and those of my friends. Disposable plastic storage became a drag in certain markets, especially in the younger, more intensely green crowd.

SC Johnson evolved Ziploc. They recognized that their true value wasn't in the bag itself. It was in easy-to-use food storage. They took their market full circle—back to the days of Tupperware. What a new face they put on good old Tupperware! Light, flexible food-storage containers that we can use and reuse. Yet it's so inexpensive we can send it home with our friends or to school with our kids. We'll just pick up more at the grocery!

Ziploc's evolution isn't an exception at SC Johnson. It's the rule. Take a look at their line of Glade air fresheners, which bring the scents of nature into our homes. The brand is synonymous with happy smells and loving times. I still remember the smell of Spring Bouquet in my Nana's living room.

Glade scents originally came in aerosol sprays. But then we learned that aerosol wasn't so great for our atmosphere. So Glade evolved, packaging their signature scents in PlugIns that were more eco-friendly. With their scented oil, those little PlugIns freshen the air automatically, so our homes are always pleasant. But the market evolved. Scented candles let us enjoy the softness of candlelight, combined with our favorite scents. We gals loved the idea, and we bought a lot of candles. Suddenly, scented candles were in every boutique, and the major consumer brands were selling designer scents for every occasion.

SC Johnson saw yet another opportunity. The popular scented candles were more expensive than regular candles or PlugIns. That meant there was a segment of the market that might not want to pay the higher prices. So Glade offered their signature scents in candles, available at a much lower price point than boutique candles. We can buy them at the grocery store, the pharmacy and even some 7-Elevens. SC Johnson mapped the value of Glade—great scents at affordable prices—to a newly emerging market for candles. Then they segmented a portion of the growing candle audience to serve, and serve well.

SC Johnson is a living example of evolution that powers sustainable growth. SC Johnson knows their core value and they stay true to it. They also understand the need to evolve with changing markets. In some cases they have led the way with new and innovative approaches, such as the PlugIn. In other cases they have followed the markets to offer effective alternatives to specific market segments, such as Ziploc storage containers or Glade scented candles.

We can all evolve as SC Johnson has so successfully done. We simply need to think dynamically, focusing on evolving our value to capture the best market opportunities today, evolving as we go to capture opportunities for tomorrow.

———————

Opportunities are all around us. That's a good thing, but it also creates challenges for our business. The key is to be thoughtful as you select and then focus in on your best opportunities. Keep a constant eye out for new opportunities on your horizon, but also stay focused on your select targets. Then make a conscious and well-informed decision to evolve your focus as that new opportunity moves into your flight path. Next, let's take a look at how to identify the best Opportunity Horizon for your business.

PILOT HANDBOOK: HORIZONS OF OPPORTUNITY

1. **Opportunity is all around us.** We operate in a wide horizon of opportunity. That's why we must focus our resources on the opportunities that represent our best chance for growth.

2. **Opportunity Horizons change.** Pilots fly over a fairly static landscape—the earth rotates but doesn't move around at will. Markets are different in this respect. Marketscapes change continuously, their speed and direction determined by the inherent behaviors of business buyers, competitive alternatives, economic pressures and more. That's why you need to constantly watch your markets and adjust your course.

3. **Our Opportunity Horizon includes a variety of market segments.**

   - **Current markets** are the segments where you are successfully selling today. Expanding sales into current markets is often the easiest growth path.

   - **Complementary markets** offer the lowest-risk opportunities for business growth. They are associated in some way with current targets, requiring minimal evolution to create distinct value.

   - **Left and right field** offer breakout growth opportunities but usually require significant shifts in course, business model, offerings and your business. Taking a sudden sharp turn is not usually the best course of action—be thoughtful and plan to intercept these markets at the optimum time for your success.

   - **20/20 markets** are the ones you see after the fact, when you've already traveled in a different direction. Beware of these markets. Abruptly changing course toward these markets can disrupt your entire flight.

   - **Emerging markets** power breakout velocity. They also carry big risk. Emerging markets are the least predictable of all. Emerging markets appear from any point on your horizon. The closer an emerging market is to your current course, the easier it is to take advantage of it.

4. **Every strategic growth plan is situational.** The best relative matches between your markets and growth depend on your value, current course and your ever-changing business situation.

The Bottom Line. Opportunity Horizons change constantly. To sustainably soar, you must stay in touch with your markets, understanding where your value resonates well, sensing when that resonance begins to fade, searching for your next market opportunity. Nothing stays the same; neither should your business.

CHAPTER 17

Catch That Lift!

Match distinct value with a market that is willing to pay for that value.

So, how do we identify our best growth strategy—that is, which opportunities we'll pursue and why? First, we have to recognize the two primary sources of sustainable growth: true value and market opportunity. You can't have one without the other and expect to reach business velocity.

Value in search of a market isn't value at all. You can have the best widget ever, solving a problem that no one else can solve. But if no one is willing to pay you to solve that problem, your widget isn't really that valuable, now is it?

A market opportunity without value to fill it isn't really an opportunity. There may be opportunity need for some new service or solution, but if no one can profitably provide that service, then there's no growth opportunity.

The best growth scenarios happen when we identify value that maps across a diversity of market opportunities for today and tomorrow. It doesn't have to be the same value in the exact same form. Finding consistent core value that we can evolve to serve multiple markets gives us leverage, just as SC Johnson found with its Glade brand. When we identify such consistent value sweet spots, we can focus our investment on a narrower range of value—evolving it deeply for distinction. That's a much stronger approach than attempting to create new and distinct value for each individual market opportunity.

We've learned how to identify your value. We've discussed the concept of creating a market Opportunity Horizon. Now is the time to use those tools to identify your best market opportunities, prioritizing them to define the best routes to sustainable growth.

The key is to explore each market opportunity in depth, determining how your value currently, or in the future, can meet the needs of that market. We all already know that, right? The problem is that as we explore each market, we drag along our status quo. We apply those standard paint-by-number approaches, focusing on market size and growth to rank our opportunities.

Forget selecting market targets based solely on opportunity size. Just because a market is big and growing doesn't mean it's your best opportunity. Instead, look at your value and markets in the context of your situation today, what's coming tomorrow and—most important—based on your audience input and your pure gut instinct. From there, define a flight plan, aligning your focus toward the markets that offer optimum stability and growth given your value today, while evolving that value to address tomorrow's growth opportunities. We'll discuss how to create and execute a flight plan in the next chapter. For now, let's focus on evaluating your market opportunities.

Go Back to the Keepers

To be successful, we must gather up-to-date information from the keepers of the truth. Forget about working inside out when it comes to planning for sustainable growth. Defining strategies in the vacuum created by our own corporate legends is how gravity thrives. To reach beyond the status quo, we must invert our flight planning to begin with our business reality based on external perspectives.

I seek customer, prospect and partner feedback before I define any part of a growth strategy, Value Mix or Opportunity Horizon. Clients often ask me why I don't take their word about their specific situation concerning value and markets. It's not that I don't believe them. I do. It's that I don't believe any of us clearly see our reality in the same way as our audiences. We're too busy managing our operations and focusing on our own worlds.

I collect a variety of inputs on each market before I prioritize my opportunities and create a route map. A blend of tangible and intangible information allows you to make the most informed strategic decisions, matching your value to markets that are willing to pay for that value.

Tangible Input

Tangible data can give you a place to start with each opportunity segment. But numbers in and of themselves aren't enough. Follow the guidelines discussed for applying tangible data in chapter 7. You can absolutely use numbers to support decisions; just don't rely on them for the whole truth.

Exactly what tangible data do you want to gather? Following are the key opportunity questions I focus on answering.

1. Is this market truly growing? How much, and where?

Gather the industry growth estimates from trusted resources. Then cross-match them with what you see in your space, as well as others' market projections. Don't just take those industry research numbers as truth. Analysts and researchers often derive their numbers from vendors themselves, which makes their data suspect. I always validate and adjust these numbers according to a variety of sources versus trusting one expert.

Aside from broad-reaching market numbers, get a feel for the growth and movement within the subsegments of each opportunity segment. For example, we may see high growth in the electronic gaming industry. But that's not much help in planning a strategy. What's important to know is where the submarket growth resides. For example, if young adults between the ages of fifteen and twenty-two account for 50 percent of that growth, there's your market target. If guys over the age of forty account for 20 percent of the growth, but gals only 5 percent, you won't be well served by focusing value development and marketing on women over forty, will you?

To create a focused market map, you must understand the behavior in the submarkets that make up an opportunity. I also use tangible data to prioritize my target timing within each segment, starting with the early or high-growth adopters and then expanding to include the later or slower adopters when the time and margins are optimal.

2. Is it still a high-value space or is it beginning to commoditize?

This is one of the most important questions to ask before you set your course for a market. As I've said before, just because a market is growing doesn't mean it's a great opportunity. Find out how mature the market has become, how the margins are trending. A smaller market with early adopters willing to pay big margins is often a much better target than a larger growth market with slim and declining margins. You need to understand the market's dynamics beyond simple growth trends to create your best strategic plan.

If the market is retaining significant margins, it's a valid opportunity. If it's starting to slide into lower margins, gather qualitative feedback around the price points associated with your value to determine expected margins. You'll then prioritize the market based on the expected returns. It may still be a great opportunity, depending on your other opportunities, the flexibility of your own cost points and your overall power in that market.

Sometimes it makes sense to target these segments because they set you up for a future market opportunity. For example, the credibility gained in this market may be valuable for the emerging market that's coming right into your line of flight. Markets do act as connections between each other, so this isn't a bad strategy. If I could win a highly visible market segment that was commoditizing but would also set me up for leadership in other complementary markets, I'd go for it. If such a market segment would not help me grow my business in the fairly near future, I'd think twice before targeting a stand-alone market with declining margins. If you're already in that market, stay until you've gotten any potential gravy out of it. Then move on.

3. What are my competitors' positions?

Don't start doing deep competitive analysis; that's not what you need. You need to know the market positions of established market leaders—if there are any. You already know your position versus alternatives in your current markets. Apply that information and evolve it to understand future opportunities in these and new market spaces. For all markets, understanding the competitive landscape is key to a decision about your strategic course and focus. Just don't follow your competitors. Think for yourself!

It's much easier to grow when you're the only game in town, or when you have the opportunity to be the biggest vendor in a space. If you're the big fish in a current market pond that's doing well, *keep selling*. Look for complementary markets with smaller competitors where you can leverage your current position for broader success. If there's an emerging market that no one has claimed—and it matches with your value—that's a prime target. You can establish leadership quickly and grow.

On the other hand, seeking growth in a crowded or fragmented market segment is not your best choice. Similarly, targeting a market where one competitor has substantial market share may not be the wisest approach for growth, unless that competitor is slipping and you have the value to capture all the business they are losing. Then it may be a ready-made growth opportunity for your and your value.

4. What are the purchasing trends?

What, specifically, is being purchased is often as important as how many widgets are being sold. Beneath that top-line sales number lies important data. Dig deeper to profile those one million widgets that were sold. That's where you will find the details that will help you grow.

- Are the buying cycles faster or slower? Are buyers purchasing repetitively or only once?
- Is there a pattern to the repetition?
- What do the bundles of products look like?
- Is there a certain configuration that's more popular than others, like that two-door versus the four-door automobile, or the larger quantity package versus the singles?

These questions are especially important if you're in a consumer-focused market, but they also apply to B2B vendors. Understanding the patterns or trends around *how* your audience buys is key to planning your growth. They may have expectations of certain packaging, product bundles, colors or more.

Matching your value and offerings to the optimum purchasing cycles, packaging and other buying behaviors will help you boost sales from the moment you enter the market. Ignoring the trends can mean you aren't the best match for the buyer, even if your value is strong. Make it easy for buyers to purchase your value in a way that's comfortable for them.

If you're entering a new market there may not be any quantitative data on trends. So go ask your audience what they think. Their perspective can give you the same core information. The same goes if there's no trending information for an established market. When in doubt, go ask your audience!

Intangible Insights

Intangible insights encompass both general audience perceptions across markets and the specific audience perceptions of our value in each individual segment. We can't focus on one without the other at this stage of our planning. That's how we get stuck in downdrafts. Gather external input, focusing on people with experience and working knowledge of your suspect markets.

Here are some questions I usually ask my keepers as I search for market.

1. What are the significant challenges and opportunities in this market?

Obviously you think there are challenges you can solve or you wouldn't have targeted this space. But don't lead with your assumptions. If you're in a B2B business, ask the experts which critical problems these business buyers are paying big bucks to resolve. If you're in a B2C market, ask where the next opportunity will most likely appear for your target customers. Where are consumers spending their dollars in this space, and what does the expert see as the next big consumer hits?

You're already starting to map your value to your markets as you discuss these challenges. Ask your keepers to validate that this market does, indeed, have an opportunity or challenge that needs your value. If there's no need for your value, stop here and move to the next opportunity. Value in search of a need is not a growth opportunity!

One of the biggest mistakes we make in our growth strategies is to assume that we can create demand in the markets we select. That takes big money and lots of time. We're better off focusing on a market that already has demand, capturing a ready-made opportunity instead of attempting to create a new market space. Yes, it's fun and exciting to create markets. It's also expensive in terms of cash, resources and time. In my experience, all those resources will create stronger returns when they are focused on capturing revenue versus creating demand, then watching as some new entrant captures the demand we created with a better widget.

2. How can my value solve these challenges or enhance these opportunities?

The experts validated that there is a problem or an opportunity. But can you really apply your value? That's the next question to ask. Share your core and segment values in relative markets with your keepers. Then ask them how they see your value matching their specific needs. Gather all the different ideas and approaches you can. Listen and learn, probe in depth into all areas, even the ones that may seem abstract. What you learn today is your fuel for tomorrow.

Keepers and experts will give you the trajectory for your course today, tomorrow and far into the future. When you get the right people focused on tuning your value in their market, it's amazing what you can learn. Sometimes they come up with ideas that are brilliant, especially if your value solves a problem near and dear to their heart. Leverage their in-depth market knowledge to brainstorm options for your value. Sometimes their ideas won't jive with your focus or capabilities. But more often than not they'll share a concept that opens a whole new course and flight plan for your business. Even a simple observation can trigger significant insights on your part. Don't just follow their lead. Listen and apply their perspectives to your own brainstorming. After all, many heads are better than one!

3. What other vendors can solve this problem (or bring this opportunity to reality)? Why and how?

You're not asking for detailed competitive analysis; you're scoping out the alternatives. Learn everything you can about who might challenge you or who has already captured the best opportunities in this particular space. If there's another vendor preparing to snatch that same market, one who can match your value, you might want to think again—*especially* if that vendor is bigger than you are. Getting into a battle as soon as you enter a space can drain resources, slow growth and leave you wondering why those profits aren't coming as quickly as expected.

Sometimes a perceived competitor is actually a potential partner for your market efforts. Not all competitors for a segment offer the same value. Perhaps they have value in areas you don't, and vice versa. Maybe you have a common competitor that you both want to overcome. Together, you are a bigger force than as individual players. Keep your eyes open and evaluate other players with an eye toward partnership, as well as competition.

4. What other industries are solving these challenges today?

You can always learn a lot from markets on a similar trajectory. Just don't apply that learning directly to your market and assume it works. Follow the concepts, but don't copy the details.

If these issues have been solved in another market, you can learn from their successes. You can also learn from their mistakes, avoiding the same assumptions or missteps. Capture examples of winning *and* losing strategies, then apply what's relevant to your own growth strategy.

New opportunities often emerge around industries that are a bit ahead of the game. You may find another target to add to your horizon. For example, in the information technology space, the early adopters are the ones who first use new applications in a real business environment. You might target a small business market segment to solve a similar issue in a market that will soon follow the early adopters. You can fine-tune your value for the needs of that smaller operation in a way that makes your value highly compelling. In so doing you'll win business in that new space by better matching their needs than the established players in the larger and more complex early-adopter space will be able to do.

5. Are there any barriers to entry?

If there's a reason you might not be successful in this market find out up front. Barriers to entry vary depending on the market and the situation.

- An entrenched and beloved market leader is a significant barrier.
- Required government certification is often a barrier.
- The cost of retooling manufacturing or creating an entire new distribution channel can be a barrier when we're short on cash.
- Buyer mistrust of new vendors is a significant barrier. Often you won't have enough lead time to win them over before you need to begin making a profit.

One of the biggest barriers to entry that I've seen many clients overlook, or try to minimize, is investment dollars. You have to carefully evaluate the investment required to chase this shiny new market. Set your limits for investing before you quantify the cost—and don't fudge on them. If the cost is higher than what you think you can afford, move on. Don't be hopeful; *be realistic*. For example, if there's a big competitor that is slipping in customer satisfaction and that's one of your values, you might create a plan to overcome the competitor's strength with a focused customer effort. But if the resources required to win customer trust are much more than you can afford, overcoming that barrier to capture the market may send your business reeling. Consider moving on to other, more compelling opportunities.

Ask the experts—internal and external—what they see as the barriers. Once you understand the potential potholes, you can reevaluate your options.

Once you gather all the information concerning your potential markets and their relative position around your value, your next step is to take a hard look at each market-to-value relationship, identifying those that offer you true opportunity and those that don't. Take the immediate step of discarding the segments that are obviously not great opportunities for you. If every market you identified falls into that category, go back and start again. Broaden your horizon and think outside the box.

JUST-SAY-NO TRIGGERS

Saying "No" is a business skill we must develop for sustainable growth. How do you recognize a not-so-great opportunity? That will depend on your business, but here are some high-level Just-Say-No triggers.

- **Entrenched competitors.** Unless you have a value that knocks everyone else out of the game, the time and investment required to enter a market with bigger, well-established players are better applied to other more available market segments. If you're already in this market and not gaining ground, start looking for other growth options.

- **Growing markets that are commoditizing.** If you can't see a substantial profit stream why bother targeting this market? Except in rare circumstances when commoditization is in play think twice before expending resources to target a declining profit opportunity.

- **Too much investment required in a cool new segment.** We all turn into cats with shiny objects at the sight of a really cool market. Don't do this! Move on to a more profitable opportunity and let the rest of your competitors duke it out for that coolest prize. They'll all devote resources to the same market while you grow in a more profitable and less competitive opportunity.

- **Not a value or business match.** Sometimes you know your value can't play and win in a segment. Stop with the wishful thinking and maybes. Move on.

Aligning Your Value and Opportunity to Power Growth

The best growth strategy depends on the situation.

The next step is to align your current value with your market opportunities to identify how that value may need to evolve, what type of evolution is possible and which opportunities should be prioritized over others.

This requires situational analysis. Every strategy is unique. That's why creating a growth strategy is such an art. There are no set rules.

To see this process in action, let's take a look at BizTech and their Opportunity Horizon. Remember that in chapter 10 I described the Value Mix they defined when I first began working with them. The Opportunity Horizon that follows shows the somewhat broad focus they originally believed to be their best market opportunities.

Their targeting strategy initially included:

Current markets: Focused on the SMB in specific industries.

Complementary markets: Enterprise accounts in those same industry sectors.

Left and right field markets: BizTech viewed any expansion into new SMB opportunities as a distraction from their bigger target—the enterprise. In fact, they were planning on turning their SMB customers and prospects over to an in-house telesales team to manage going forward.

As you probably recall, that Opportunity Horizon didn't match with their value. And it didn't match what we learned about their market opportunities either.

We gathered both tangible and intangible data about each of these markets, which resulted in a thirty-page document. Let's just review some of the high-level, critical input we collected.

- The enterprise space was more than 80 percent saturated with computing systems that were viable alternatives to the new systems BizTech

BizTech Initial Opportunity Horizon

SMB
Expansion
Markets

Enterprise

New SMB
Accounts

SMB Markets
- Manufacturing
- Financial Services
- Healthcare
- Consumer Goods

Flight Path

Enterprise

SMB
Expansion
Markets

was introducing. That meant the company, in most cases, would have to replace current vendors' systems to win new business. Their value had to be really distinct and compelling. A few markets in the enterprise sector were still available to BizTech, but the value requirements for these buyers were very different from those of the SMB market.

- On the other hand, the SMB space was less than 30 percent saturated. Only early adopters and leading markets had applied computing to their businesses at this stage. That meant the majority of SMB opportunities were still available.

- The traditional SOHO and smaller markets that BizTech served were also growth opportunities, but in a very limited fashion. They wanted packaged, off-the-shelf solutions that required no complex installation or management.

- A number of new market opportunities—fueled by the Internet and web-based sales—were entering the SMB marketplace. Many of these businesses were always looking for new and innovative computing solutions.

- A number of services businesses were likewise entering the marketplace to support the enterprise accounts that BizTech wanted to target. These services businesses needed simple computing systems to manage their customer relationships and project applications, which were the same applications that some of BizTech's current customers used.

- Eight out of ten vendors in this computing space were targeting the enterprise. That made for a pretty crowded marketplace. Only one out of ten was offering solutions packaged for the SOHO and lower-end SMB, and those solutions offered limited capabilities. Sounds like an opportunity to me!

- Fortune 500 buyers were adamant about their loyalty to large established vendors in the market.

Based on this feedback, we realigned BizTech's market Opportunity Horizon to focus on high-value, repeatable and available targets where they could grow successfully.

We made some pretty significant changes to their original growth plan. Yes, enterprise customers are a target, but they are not an easy target to address. There were much easier, readily available targets in the current SMB marketplace. BizTech initially wanted to go for the bright-lights market in the enterprise. The enterprise segment represents the Holy Grail for so many computing vendors, even though it's not a great market for many. Once again, following the competition and going for the popular opportunity can send us into a downward spiral even as we ignore the fuel that could send us soaring toward growth.

Now, let's look at how we aligned BizTech's Value Mix and evolved Opportunity Horizon to prioritize a strategy that will effectively power sustainable growth.

BizTech Evolved Value Mix

Value Mix	Core Value	Segment Value
Company	Simple business computing	SMB committed 3 decades of SMB experience 200+ happy SMB customers
Product	It just works!	Simple computing saves money Designed to keep your business going
Market	We help make SMBs successful	We understand SMB We save SMBs money We help SMBs grow

As you'll recall, BizTech's evolved Value Mix focused on the SMB marketplace, so we aligned it directly with our market opportunities. In this case, we have a set of core values that apply across all SMB opportunities. This is the ideal case we discussed earlier. All of our product value evolution can be focused on the common needs of our market, with different packaging creating the distinct value we want to offer to specific segments, based on their individual needs.

At the highest level, what did we see as the matches between BizTech's value and their opportunities?

- BizTech was a recognized leader in a growing, high-opportunity market (SMB).

- The enterprise market was overcrowded; BizTech was not a known vendor and their new product value wasn't perceived to be a fit for that space today.

- Their new product was a fit for the enterprise, but it was going to be a tough sell given the barriers to entry we uncovered. SMB audiences didn't really need or want the new product, so it didn't hold value in their eyes.

Based on BizTech's evolved Value Mix, we evolved to a new Opportunity Horizon.

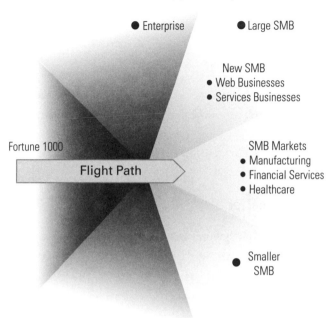

BizTech's Evolved Opportunity Horizon

As you can see, BizTech's key focus is on the SMB marketplace, with a variety of SMB segments identified as targets. SMBs represent the kind of growth opportunity we would all love to have. Huge growth potential with minimal investment in a market we already own. How's that for a winner?

Following are more details around the specific target segments in Biz-Tech's Opportunity Horizon.

1. Expand current targets.

The company had in excess of five hundred customers in the SMB market. It's a no-brainer for BizTech to seek growth within that customer base and with targets whose profiles are similar to current customers. Why? It's always easier to grow by leveraging a current customer base than it is to go after new opportunities. It's also easier to grow by targeting buyers with profiles that are similar to your current customers. You can leverage your market value (in the form of customer referrals) to quickly capture new, yet similar audiences.

2. New SMB opportunities.

The high-growth opportunity for new SMB players in the web and services businesses was a complementary market. These were leading-edge companies who were growing their information needs by leaps and bounds. Yet they also wanted a simple, just-works solution.

3. Packages for smaller SMBs.

Those smaller SMBs that haven't adopted systems are also a great opportunity for growth. By capturing them, BizTech can solidify its position as *the* SMB-friendly company. And as BizTech grows, those smaller SMBs will continue to buy more systems, which powers continuing revenue. That's great news all around. BizTech just needed to make a few changes in its product packaging to address their needs more efficiently.

4. Enterprise strategy.

Enterprise accounts were not a great fit for the current product or the company's current status. But the new product value was focused more on large SMBs or low-end enterprises. So we needed a longer-term plan to penetrate the enterprise space. Either that or we needed to ditch the new product, which the company and its investors were not willing to do given the huge investment that had been made. We isolated the efforts around the enterprise market to avoid distracting the rest of the SMB-focused teams, creating a plan for test flights that would not disrupt the main focus on SMB.

5. Keep core focus on the SMB.

The very idea that BizTech might move to the enterprise market was a turn-off to current SMB customers and new prospects. So we stopped the public conversations about the enterprise. We focused marketing and brand efforts on positioning the company as the leader—the *only* leader—in the SMB computing space. Any revenue we gained in enterprise sales was upside—and paid for the investment in the new product. We were using some of the new product features to fuel new versions of the current systems—creating the opportunity for significant upgrade revenue associated with profitable margins.

BizTech was ready to make a mistake that's pretty common. They saw a bright-light market in the enterprise—one that has more excitement, more notoriety and a huge opportunity—and they changed their value course to tackle it. It's obvious now that wasn't their best growth strategy. But at the time I met them, they hadn't yet realized it. Their belief in that huge opportunity was a big source of gravity. If they'd pursued it, they would have almost certainly crashed and burned.

———————

Continuous, dependable growth comes through focusing on what's best for your business at any point in time. Opportunity markets must match your value for you to be successful. Following the rest of the pack to compete in the most popular markets will not necessarily result in growth. Sometimes, it can be just the gravity to take you down. That's why every decision has to be based on your situation—not on what everyone else is doing.

You must also keep a keen eye on your markets, evolving your focus when complementary and emerging new opportunities come into alignment with your flight. You can't settle for one source of lift and expect to grow forever.

Now that you understand how to align your value with your markets to identify your best growth strategy, the next step is to create your flight plan.

PILOT HANDBOOK: CATCH THAT LIFT!

1. **Businesses grow when we match value with a market that is willing to pay for that value.** There are two primary sources of sustainable growth: true value and market opportunity. You can't have one without the other and expect to reach full business velocity.

2. **Carefully evaluate each opportunity.** A blend of tangible and intangible inputs is necessary for an informed decision about your best opportunities.

   - **Tangible** input includes market growth trends, competitive market shares, specific buying trends and your own market position.

   - **Intangible** insights come from experts in each segment and include value perceptions, unsolved problems that match your value, the trust and position of other vendors, barriers to entry and similar industries that you can pattern. Intangible insights help you begin to align your value with your markets—the first step in prioritizing your flight plan.

3. **Turn away from opportunities with minimal chance of success.** There's no reason to waste time and effort on an opportunity that's difficult when you have lots of opportunities that you can capture in a straightforward way. Some signs of a problem opportunity include:

   - **Entrenched competitors.** Find a market that's more open and available. Fighting a battle with an entrenched vendor can be a huge resource drain, and it has little chance of success unless you have a very powerful value along with the resources to create awareness.

   - **Growing markets that are commoditizing.** Why go into a market that's already lost its profit edge? Better to find a market that's still value priced, unless there's no other choice. Then, look for ways to add value to increase those margins.

   - **Too much investment required.** Sure it's a bright and shiny space—like the enterprise was for BizTech. But the resources and changes required to capture customers—from product value to the fundamentals of the company itself—are too big to warrant the risk.

- **Not a value or business match**. If the shoe doesn't fit, find one that does. There are lots of choices. If there aren't, you need to reevaluate your business.

4. **The best growth strategy depends on the situation**. Forget the paint-by-number approaches; they don't work in today's dynamic markets. Every strategy is unique and requires situational analysis. There are no set rules.

The Bottom Line. Select opportunities that match your value, have minimal entrenched competitors and offer attractive growth—and where you have a realistic chance to win.

CHAPTER 13

Planning Go-to-Market Routes

The more leveraged your go-to-market routes, the better your chance to grow.

Pilots focus on successfully flying one route, following its landmarks and sometimes flying to a connecting destination before reaching their ultimate end-point. We can do the same in business.

We do have more than one go-to-market route, since we usually target multiple market segments. But we still need to focus. We can't simultaneously set out for every opportunity market we've identified. Not unless we have unlimited resources, which is rarely the case. We must prioritize and focus.

Unfortunately, our traditional approaches often set us up for faulty execution planning. The Way We've Always Done It explains how status quo planning can get us into trouble. Thanks to that bit of status quo, changing the way we tactically plan and execute our growth strategy is just as important as changing the way we think about and create those strategies.

The Way We've Always Done It

Traditional planning causes us to try to do too much, or the wrong combination of things, with limited resources. The former spreads us too thin; the latter leaves holes in our value as we address our markets.

We do have a logical reason for doing too much. If we take on everything, we can spread our risk in case we fail in one area. Unfortunately, that means we end up doing everything with less quality and focus. That's not a winning strategy. Focus and discipline solve this problem.

We also have a reason for doing the wrong things. It's called our *planning process*. We make a list of our top priority value enhancements—for example, new product features. Each value enhancement is then prioritized as a stand-alone entity instead of in relation to its market segment(s). We apply resources to those enhancements. When we reach the end of our available resources, we draw a line—and *that's our value plan*.

Review the Traditional Planning Approach below. The priorities are focused on individual, tactical value enhancements, with an arbitrary line drawn based on available resources.

Example: Traditional Planning Approach

Value Enhancement	Resources Required	Cost
New product features into current product	2 man-years	$240,000
Large SMB product upgrades	1 man-year	$120,000
Web-focused product upgrades	5 man-months	$50,000
Services-focused product upgrades	4 man-months	$40,000
Package product for SOHO	1 man-year	$120,000
Small enterprise sales team	3 man-years	$360,000
Application support for Small Enterprise	1 man-year	$120,000
Seamless product upgrade capability	2 man-months	$20,000
Channel Program 4 SOHO	2 man-years + OPEX	$400,000
Application focus for new SMB customers with upgraded current product	6 man-months	$60,000
Starter system for SMB	2 man-months	$24,000

These priorities are not based on providing the complete value required for each target segment. When we use this planning approach, we don't develop the comprehensive required value to be successful in any market segment. We deliver pieces of value across all segments then make up for the value holes by discounting or other means. That is not a growth strategy—it's a plan for buying time.

Go-to-Market Routes

Strategic routes create comprehensive, highly leveraged paths to success.

Flight plans factor in such details as fuel capacity, weight and airspeeds. They also plot the routes to a destination, including departure points, landmarks along the way, navigational aids, headings and distances.

Our business flight plan includes similar information.

Value, your fuel, represents the departure point for your business flight. Your future value represents incremental opportunities for thrust and momentum along your route. Value also determines your market speed. By the way, when you carry excess weight, you've increased your gravity, and it will eat away at your fuel—your value.

Markets, the destinations, may be viewed as interim destinations in a series of connecting flights or as a single ultimate market. Each destination acts either as a next step toward another destination or as an end into itself. We need to understand the interrelationships of each route and destination with the other routes and destinations on our radar to create a leveraged, evolutionary plan.

Go-to-market strategies, the routes, are a combination of your value and your markets that creates a focus for your efforts. Your go-to-market strategies for these value/market combinations represent the route your business flight will take. Each route represents certain required value evolution and operational changes, which require adequate resources to be successful.

As you create your tactical flight plans, it's important to remember that there's no need for huge leaps to reach for growth. You can leverage a series of interim destinations to reach your ultimate market. You can also change your course along the way if you see a more expedient route. You can achieve this constant evolution by using the waypoints described in the next chapter. But you have to choose your routes before you can define your waypoints.

The first goal of route planning is to evaluate segments based on resources, the availability of each market and ultimate business returns. We then identify go-to-market routes that deliver immediate success in initial target segments while also building leverage—in the form of company, product and market value—to accelerate our success into our expanded yet related opportunity segments.

These are the steps I use to define optimum routes with my clients.

1. Define the complete value required for your success in each target segment.

The way to capture leadership in an opportunity segment is to focus on delivering *all* the required value. You must prioritize your resource investments based on meeting the complete needs of each target segment, not based on discrete pieces of value or the easiest, lowest cost value to evolve.

How do you group and prioritize value evolution and map it to segments?

- First, make a list of all the required value evolutions required to be successful across all market segments.

- Next, calculate the resources and costs associated with each unique value evolution. To be thorough, include both soft and hard costs.

- Finally, group the value evolutions (and their costs/resources) based on each market segment they serve. Some value enhancements may play within multiple markets. That's a good thing because it creates leverage for any investment in that value evolution. Make note of such values that have cross-market applications. Those specific value enhancements will receive higher priority, assuming they play in priority opportunity segments.

The resulting value groupings represent the required bundle of value you need for success in each specific market opportunity.

For example, if the new SMB market opportunity for BizTech requires evolution in multiple product values, a slightly evolved company value and additional market value in the form of specific customer referrals, group those requirements together as a single value bundle. Either fully invest in the resources for that entire bundle or choose another bundle and market. I usually recommend clients invest in value bundles for priority markets first. Once those value bundles are delivered, you can move rapidly into those markets; at the same time, you can begin to create the next value bundle for your next priority market segment.

Once you have all the values grouped for each market, summarize the resources required for each market bundle. You'll use this summary to prioritize your routes in the next step.

In the sidebar, you'll see a map of value, markets and required resources for BizTech. In this case, we slowed our movement into the small enterprise space until we had the resources and budget we needed. In the meantime, we began the value evolutions required for the top three priority markets, which were highly leveraged one to another. Only when we were moving forward with a complete value bundle for each of these markets did we realign our resources to focus on the outlying market opportunity—small enterprise.

2. Prioritize your go-to-market routes.

Moving forward on each market route simultaneously isn't usually the best strategy for growth—unless you happen to have unlimited resources. We can't do it all. We need to prioritize based on available resources, expected returns, the power of our value and the relationship between these markets that we can leverage.

The choices you make concerning your route priorities depend on your situation. You have to continually reevaluate your markets, as we discussed in chapter 12. For example:

If you're already winning in a high-growth market with a high-value product, think about limiting your investment in that product and beginning to evolve to meet the needs of the next destination on your route. If you're already a leader and doing well, leverage that leadership position while focusing time and resources on growing in another area. Don't

Value Enhancement by Market	Resources Required	Cost
Current SMB Expansion		
Product Value: New product features into current product	2 man-years	$240,000
Product Value: Seamless product upgrade capability	2 man-months	$20,000
Product Value: Application focus for new SMB customers with upgraded current product	6 man-months	$60,000
Web and Services SMB		
Product Value: Web-focused product upgrades	5 man-months	$50,000
Product Value: Services-focused product upgrades	4 man-months	$40,000
Market Value: Marketing to web SMBs		$75,000
Company Value: Training to sell web SMBs		$25,000
Market Value: Referral customer focus		$25,000
Small Business		
Product Value: Package product for Small Biz	1 man-year	$120,000
Market Value: Channel Program for Small Biz	2 man-years + OPEX	$400,000
Product Value: Starter system for SMB	2 man-months	$24,000
Company Value: Small Biz awareness		$75,000
Small Enterprise		
Market Value: Small enterprise sales team	3 man-years	$360,000
Product Value: Large SMB product upgrades	1 man-year	$120,000
Product Value: Application support for small enterprise	1 man-year	$120,000
Company Value: Enterprise awareness		$100,000

continue to dump more resources into a product that's winning. If you have a significantly sustainable differentiation, enjoy it and expand your focus. Find a market that needs a few focused value extensions where you can be successful. Support that effort with some of the resources from your high-value and already leading product offering. It's a more balanced approach to growth.

If profits in your current market are commoditizing—think about investing elsewhere sooner rather than later. Learning to evolve when our current course begins to decline in momentum is one of the best lessons we can all learn. Is there a complementary market where your value plays well with little evolution? Begin to invest there. Use a submarket of that segment to run a test flight, tuning your value and approach until it's highly compelling. Then broaden your focus to the entire segment.

If you have five successful markets and not enough resources to go around to advance in all of them, it's better to pick the largest profit (not revenue) opportunities instead of trying to do it all. Don't spread yourself too thin. Focus.

Evaluate your options, being sure to avoid the status quo that's sure to rise in your analysis. Then select the best combination of routes based on your value today, your best market opportunities and the resources you have available to meet each market's needs. Don't try to target a market with only part of the value required; you'll crash and burn. That failure can impact your future success in other markets as well. Bad news travels fast and far.

3. Align your route maps for optimum leverage.

Optimum routes allow you to leverage success in near-term market segments, or subsegments, to accelerate your success in longer-term segments. You can also establish routes into new markets that leverage test flights, gathering the value you need to create success before you move into the broader segment.

Leverage is found within single segments or across multiple segments. Let's review a couple of examples of leveraged routes.

By using test flights and interconnected routes when you enter that first smaller subsegment, you'll learn whether you've made a mistake in your choice of route or destination. You can realign your thinking and evolve to a better route. You don't have to make it work no matter what. You can accept that business and markets do change and move on to a better opportunity that's already in your sights.

That's one of the reasons I suggest clients keep track of all their targets. You never know when one of those markets will align itself directly in front of your current course, or when you'll need to move to the next market on your Opportunity Horizon. Keep your focus on your priorities, but keep a watchful eye on your suspect markets. Market dynamics can change so quickly that you need to be able to quickly realign your routes. By keeping track of your Opportunity Horizon, you'll be ready with all the information you need to make a strong decision about your next best course.

> Adopting go-to-market routes also eliminates the need to try to do it all.

Let's look again at BizTech to see how to apply the above steps in the real world.

Route Planning in Action—BizTech

Here are the four routes with associated priorities and execution plans that we created for BizTech.

Route #1: Current SMB Markets. This route deepens sales within our current customers, while targeting prospects who share common profiles with our customer base. This route represents BizTech's current course, which has been expanded to include more targets.

- The company invested millions in its new product offering. We used that new product's applicable value to enhance the current product offering. We offered it to the entire customer base (as well as new targets) as a transitional system between their current and new products.

BizTech Go-to-Market Routes

We created an easy method for customers to leverage key value from the new product that they needed today in a simple and much less disruptive fashion than moving to the entire new product.

- We offered a complete upgrade to the new product for select large SMB accounts. We targeted those SMBs who shared similar needs to small enterprises in health-care and retail. In the process, we gathered referrals for our new product within those small enterprise target markets.

- We also defined an outreach strategy to SMB prospects. We focused heavily on mapping current customer applications to these new target profiles, leveraging BizTech's outstanding market value within SMB.

Route #2: New SMB Markets. New web and services SMBs offered the highest opportunity for growth with the least investment. In this case, we created a test flight into this new segment, where BizTech was relatively unknown. We leveraged select customer testimonials to successfully sell to a highly influential group of new customers during our test flight. We in turn leveraged their market support to fuel our entry to the mainstream web and services segment. We also gathered expertise and credibility in this space.

- We then defined a new system, leveraging both the current and the new product values that specifically met the customers' need for rapidly growing information and always-on service levels.

- We selected a small group of web and services businesses to capture as initial referrals for the mainstream web and services market. We didn't go after broad targets: we focused on twenty accounts. Those accounts became the target for a small focused group of sales reps we selected for their specific expertise in this space. We created a focused sales strategy before turning these reps loose. Within four months, these reps won ten of the twenty accounts. We also tuned up the sales approach to accelerate time-to-revenue.

- Once we captured the initial customers, we leveraged those referrals to target an expanded audience with similar profiles, focusing on higher-profit opportunities first. We moved to target smaller accounts later—after we put in place a streamlined, lower-cost sales strategy. We leveraged a combination of inside and outside sales teams for efficiency with these smaller accounts.

Route #3: Packaged SMB. BizTech's third priority was to capture the opportunity found in smaller SMBs. In this case, we needed a bit of value evolution, both in our product and our channels.

- We selected a small team with backgrounds in defining and packaging ready-to-run systems. The result offered simple, basic functionality in a system that was easy to install and use and was affordable as well. We targeted this system toward the small SMB and SOHO marketplace.

- We entered into an agreement with three large channel partners to provide this system to their smaller business customers. BizTech didn't have to create a new channel, saving precious dollars and time.

- A version of this system was also packaged as a starter system for larger SMBs that had not yet moved to automated operations. BizTech offered this package to its new channels as well, giving them an opportunity to sell to larger SMB accounts, increasing the return on investment they made in BizTech and strengthening the partnership.

Route #4: Small Enterprise. BizTech didn't want to give up on the enterprise entirely; there were a number of small enterprise segments we believed we could capture with the new product offering. But we needed credibility and experience in this space before BizTech began to address it head-on. We spearheaded a separate effort to prepare for the enterprise.

- We defined a short list of current customers who were large SMB accounts in health-care and retail. These customers represented our connecting route to get to the enterprise. We selected/hired a small group of field sales, service and support personnel who understood these industries. We focused their efforts on upgrading these SMB accounts to the new product, at minimal disruption to their customers. These accounts became the Proof of Concept and reference accounts we would need as BizTech began to address smaller enterprise accounts. We also used these accounts to tune up the new product, making sure it was stable and reliable for the enterprise before BizTech moved to address that space.

- We partnered with two large application vendors—one from each industry. These partners already enjoyed the trust of the enterprise accounts. BizTech worked with these vendors to define a system that matched the needs of smaller enterprise accounts (closer to BizTech's SMB heritage). The credibility of these vendors, combined with Biz-Tech's large SMB account references, opened the door for sales of the new product into the small enterprise.

- It took BizTech a year to capture its first small enterprise sale. We had the product locked down for large SMB and small enterprise needs, we had the sales strategy tuned for quick results, and we had strong partner allies. We didn't take over the entire enterprise space, but we did solidify BizTech's position as a leader in the large SMB market as part of these efforts, blocking the larger enterprise competitors from moving down-market into our space.

We focused immediate efforts on the SMB markets of (a) current customers, (b) new web and services SMBs and (c) packaged SMB products. Those markets had overlapping requirements for value, which meant we leveraged our resources across all of these opportunities. They were also the most readily available to us. We focused the majority of our resources there to establish growth routes in the most streamlined manner possible.

You can create the best strategic growth plan ever, yet still fail thanks to a poor tactical go-to-market plan. Traditional approaches to resource planning and market entry often send us into the market without the focus we need to succeed. By planning the optimum routes for your go-to-market execution, you assure you have the right value for your best opportunities today, as you create a foundation for leverage tomorrow.

PILOT HANDBOOK: PLANNING GO-TO-MARKET ROUTES

1. **The more leveraged your go-to-market routes, the better your chance to grow.** Carefully plan and prioritize your go-to-market routes to best use your resources today, capturing success in key segments as leverage for tomorrow.

2. **Doing too much or the wrong things limits growth.** The former spreads you too thin; the latter leaves holes in your value as you address wide-reaching markets.

3. **Change the way you tactically plan and execute go-to-market routes.**

   - **Deliver the complete value required in each market segment.** Entering a market with incomplete value is not a plan for growth.

   - **Prioritize your go-to-market routes.** Moving forward on each market route simultaneously isn't usually the best strategy. Prioritize based on available resources, expected returns, the power of your value and the relationship between markets that offer the best leverage.

   - **Map routes for optimum leverage.** Leverage is found within single segments or across multiple segments. A route to a new market requires a test flight to gather experience and credibility before you address the mainstream segment. Market segments are often interconnected, offering leverage for successful routes from one segment to the next. Leverage interconnected markets for accelerated growth.

4. **Adopting an evolutionary approach eliminates the need to try to do it all.** By using test flights, you'll know quickly if you've made a mistake in your choice: be it due to your value, the market itself or extraneous factors. If your test flight unearths difficulties, realign your thinking and evolve to a better approach or an entirely new route.

The Bottom Line. Go-to-market routes are a critical part of executing a growth plan. Defining and executing highly leveraged and logical routes is a key to accelerating and sustaining business velocity and ongoing growth. Be thoughtful as you create and prioritize your routes. The more leverage the better.

CHAPTER 14

Evolving for Sustainable Growth

Staying on course requires continuously evolving our flight.

Pilots actively monitor their flights, making small changes as needed to optimize their flight path. The same goes for our business as we continuously streamline and evolve our course to reach for growth.

But how do we continuously update and evolve? Won't it take too long and be too resource intensive if we constantly review our value and market, our gravity and course? We need to focus on the business, not constant planning.

Those are all valid comments. They're also based on the way we've always done it. When we change the way we think about growth and change, these protests become moot. We've discussed how we need to adapt the way we think about strategy and go-to-market execution.

We must also change the way we manage and monitor our business flight, making small adjustments that bring big results. Change in the form of Big Bang reactions is replaced by change in the form of proactive evolution. We can do just that when we have the right tools in place.

But before we begin to set measurements for our progress, we must share our plan with our entire team. The only way to stay on our optimum course is to have everybody involved in monitoring our route and recommending changes when needed. Once our teams are on board, we can implement simple tools—waypoints and trim tabs—to help us identify whether we're veering off course. As our markets evolve, we can make smart adjustments in real time rather than big changes after we begin to lose our forward momentum.

All Hands on Deck

Standard operating procedure says to create a strategy and a flight plan at the executive level, then roll it out to employees, gather feedback and move on. Too often we share a vision as a *fait accompli*—that is, a dictate handed down from the executives on high. We force change, we meet resistance and we get stuck in gravity. Those old approaches bog us down, resulting in turmoil, conflict and lost productivity.

In today's dynamic market, we must retrain our teams to think about and execute change as continuous, incremental evolution. When we teach our teams to think differently about change, we have a much better chance of growing successfully.

First, share your flight plan and go-to-market routes with the company as a whole. Then ask managers to work with their teams on two steps.

Eliminate the gravity. Just as you followed the exercises in section I to eliminate the gravity in your management perspectives, do the same with employees within your business. If someone has a hard time releasing his or her gravity as you discuss your new or evolved approaches, he or she may very well be a prime source of disruption later in your flight. Face it and note it. If the resistance doesn't disappear in a reasonable time frame, take action.

Focus forward. Turn your attention to creating the detailed plans for your new flight. Use the exercises at the end of section II to discuss planning for growth. Get everyone's perspectives on the table first. Then, wherever the team's focus differs from the executive plan, ask your managers to work to align perspectives within the team. Don't shove the new plan down their throats as a done deal. Ask questions, point out potential issues and lead the team to think along the paths that you have pinpointed as your best strategic course.

- Listen for dissension, and if you can't eliminate it make note. You'll have to be aware of the potential for fragmentation later in your flight.
- Listen to team members' questions and concerns and their new ideas. Make note of all the ideas that can potentially make your flight plan even more powerful.

- Listen to the team's off-the-wall ideas. You never know when that next opportunity may bounce off that wall right into your lap.
- Listen for valid counterarguments—especially from the folks who deal with your keepers of the truth on a daily basis. They may just know something you or the executive team doesn't. Be sure and bring up all of these ideas before any strategy is deemed final.

Spend the time up front to bring your team into the new ways of thinking about and seeing your business. Also, listen to their responses and evolve your plan accordingly. Then share with them the final flight plan and the specific organizational roles and priorities they each must focus on to ensure business success. When you successfully make the change in thinking, growth becomes much easier.

A shared flight plan will make or break your success. One of the key aspects of any successful flight is making sure everyone is on the same route and having all the right skills in place.

A Square Peg in a Round Hole

You will also need to evaluate skill sets. Do you have the skill sets you need to support your flight plan? Map the expertise you need for success with the skill sets present in your organization. Define the gaps, carefully and thoughtfully. Then put a plan in place to hire the skills and experience you need to be successful.

One of the biggest mistakes I see clients make is assuming that they can retrain current employees to meet the needs of a new course and strategy. Sometimes we can retrain skills, particularly when our change in course is minor. But even then we need experts to guide our efforts in new markets or value delivery. Assuming that an expert in SMB markets can define an enterprise product is a big mistake, just as assuming a researcher focused on makeup can shift to creating perfume. They require different skills.

BizTech hired a number of enterprise experts to craft their new product offering. BizTech initially assumed that these enterprise product experts could easily define the best version of their new product to meet SMB needs. After all, these were the experts who built that product. But that didn't mean they were skilled to revamp it for SMB buyers. Anything but. In the end, BizTech released some of the enterprise experts in a fair and equitable way. They used the funding to hire SMB experts for the new SMB market segments associated with the new product focus.

Businesses also need experienced executive leadership. If your executives don't have deep experience in your opportunity markets, take a hard look at your chances of success. If you don't want to lose an executive, hire consultants or other experts to support him or her to gather on-the-job experience through executing your plan. Just don't expect that executive to find his or her own way and reach the level of expertise you need. That's asking too much, and it opens the door for gravity to drastically limit your growth.

New channels were critical for BizTech to expand its reach and range. Their direct sales executives had minimal experience in channel development. After a channel program managed by direct sales teams failed, they hired a consultant to define and execute their channel plan, along with two highly experienced channel business development managers. New channels were on board and beginning to sell within four months, with a full complement of channels powering profitable revenue within a year.

Trying to retrain your employees with new skill sets is a valiant and honorable goal. Unfortunately, it also limits your growth. Matching expertise to the needs of your flight is one of the hardest parts of any strategic discussion. No one wants to leave their employees behind as they evolve. But sometimes that's exactly what you must do if you are to soar to continued success and growth.

The Tools Make the Difference

You've developed your plan, shared it with your team and adapted it based on their feedback. The next step is to define a business-wide execution plan. Tactical plans come in all forms; the structure doesn't really matter. A number of great project management approaches are available in the market. Follow whatever planning structure works best for your organization.

There are two tools I find critical for clarifying your execution plan, monitoring your flight and making adjustments along the way. These are waypoints and trim tabs. Since these tools aren't specifically included in traditional project management approaches, add them as part of whatever approach you choose.

Pilots rely on waypoints to know where they are in relation to their original plan and to know when they need to change course for an optimum flight. Sometimes they reach a waypoint and adjust their course to a new heading. If they change course to avoid a sudden headwind, downdraft or storm, they may use new waypoints to guide them toward their destination.

Pilots use trim tabs to optimize and streamline their flight. Trim tabs reduce pilots' workloads during continuous maneuvers, allowing them to focus their attention on more important tasks than maintaining stability. Trim tabs allow for a steady, stable flight, even when changes occur in course, airspeed, wind speed or any other environmental shift.

Businesses can use waypoints to monitor progress in a more granular way than traditional measures. We set waypoints at small increments along our course, reflecting the interim positions we must reach to confirm that we're on course and making progress. By monitoring our waypoints closely, we know where we are in relation to our flight plan. When we need to adjust based on a shifting waypoint, we use trim tabs to enact steady, continuous evolution while maintaining a stable flight.

Using waypoints and trim tabs helps us continuously evolve as we move along the flight route, eliminating the need for any more Big Bangs. These tools also act as a means to continuously analyze our value and market opportunities. Once you create your initial strategy, waypoints and trim tabs make it easy to adjust to changes in your marketscape and to choose new routes when necessary.

Waypoints—Our Milestones to Growth

> Second star to the right, and straight on till morning.
> —Peter Pan

Think of waypoints as a version of the critical success milestones we've all used in business. Waypoints do include traditional milestones, such as checking quarterly results. Waypoints also include smaller and shorter-term measurements. We continuously check waypoints to assure our course is true. For example, hiring that key skill set we need to create a packaged product for the SOHO marketplace.

When we manage by waypoints, we pay closer attention to our progress on a weekly, sometimes even daily, basis. Each team has its own set of waypoints, as does each group, organization and division—all of which culminate in the top-level waypoints of the business.

Waypoints are real-world, achievable measurements of small incremental progress toward our destination. The right waypoints ensure the successful execution of our overall plan—even when changes must occur. The wrong waypoints can give us a false sense of security or a misguided belief that we're on track when we really aren't.

Don't fudge when it comes to defining your waypoint measurements. That hopeful sales number you might just make if you're really lucky is not a valid waypoint; it's a pie-in-the-sky SWAG that doesn't effectively measure your progress.

When appropriately defined, waypoints act as landmarks along our flight. Waypoints help us make sure that the markets we've targeted are still in alignment with our trajectory and that our value evolution is in lockstep with our targets. Waypoints also act as opportunities to check in on our suspect markets' course, checking to see if they've moved into closer alignment with our current trajectory.

> If a market doesn't respond as you assumed in your plan, you have a market shift.

One point to note: when we manage by waypoints, we have to be honest about our results. That means we must eliminate the excuses for why we didn't meet a given waypoint. We have to face up to what's really true about our forward progress. If you catch yourself missing a waypoint and assuring everyone it's not a big deal, you might want to check for gravity in your thinking. Assuming you planned the waypoint to reflect requirements for your success, missing that waypoint is a sign that you're off course. It may only need a tiny correction. But pay attention. Step up and adjust your plan accordingly if you did, indeed, miss a critical waypoint.

A pilot wouldn't miss a waypoint and assume she was still headed for her intended direction. She would check and double-check, then realign to meet her next waypoint.

Businesses need to do the same. Waypoints are great markers to tell us when we need a minor course adjustment, a different expectation on timing of results or maybe, a more significant rethinking of our plan. If one organization or team misses a waypoint, it affects the entire business. Be serious about the detailed and high-level markers of your progress.

Which Waypoints Are the Best?

That depends on your flight plan and your ability to execute. Each set of waypoints will be different for each business, even for each route you are following. Following are some examples of waypoints to help you create your own markers.

Value waypoints mark progress as you evolve your value to meet the needs of your markets. By monitoring these requirements for success, you have the opportunity to adjust your plan and actions ahead of any major shortfall and to capitalize on accelerated results.

Company value waypoints focus on any changes you must make at the company level. These waypoints include soft external markers, such as audience awareness and brand recognition, and internal markers related to organizational evolution, financial results and growth. Sometimes many changes are required, so you'll have a number of markers, including hiring the skill sets you need for new markets, evolving or creating that market's perception of your company and increasing your credibility as a viable, trusted vendor.

Sometimes your company value is already aligned with your market focus, which is the best-case scenario. The only markers you need are for financial results—as in the case of BizTech. We didn't need to change the company value for SMBs. Our waypoints focused on assuring that the company met its expected financial results. We focused on monitoring the expected revenue and profit from each market, as well as the sales results from each route we were flying. We also monitored sales progress in the form of time-to-revenue and close rates along each route, using these measures as early indicators of our progress toward corporate-wide financial waypoints.

Product value waypoints include both the planning milestones for evolving your value within each market and the results milestones to show that you're profitably selling each product as expected. For BizTech, we had many more product waypoints than company value waypoints. We had three separate market routes, so we created value waypoints for each of them.

Each route included waypoints for product evolution requirements, sales metrics for each product offering by market, and customer feedback to assure that we were evolving in the best direction. (This included a quick competitive overview to confirm that our value was, indeed, distinct.)

Market value waypoints help you keep an eye on your market power as it builds (or doesn't) in each target segment. I use a simple waypoint measurement for clients: the number of customers willing to provide referrals and case studies for my client. If we're doing a good job, clients will help us through referrals, quotes and full-blown case studies. Yes, I know, customers won't let us use their company name. That's okay. If they'll do a blind case study—no names and camouflaged for privacy—that's almost as good. My point is, if you aren't increasing your market power by gathering more supporters along your course, something isn't working as well as it could. Find out why the buyers aren't happy enough with their results to support you with references. By monitoring this waypoint, you can sense a problem ahead of a larger impact—and resolve it.

For example, with BizTech we set a goal of five referral customers for the new product within six months. At the end of six months, we had two referrals, but they weren't passionate. When we dug deeper, we found that the two customers were willing to do the referrals as a favor for the VP of Services who was their friend. What does that tell you? We learned there were a few installation and services issues we needed to resolve. We did just that—ahead of moving more broadly into the market. That test flight waypoint helped us avoid a significant false start in the mainstream market.

Opportunity waypoints act as external checkpoints of your target and suspect markets. These are *not* the same as your own market value waypoints. Market waypoints monitor real-world dynamics of market evolution around value needs, uptake of products, price points and growth of opportunity. These waypoints ensure that you're in sync with the needs of the markets in your flight path.

Opportunity waypoints are also used to monitor suspect markets that may just cross your course or that you may decide to steer toward depending on results in your current route. That market may have gone in a different direction or changed speed. Find out what happened and then decide whether you need to define a new waypoint. If you do change your market waypoints, check your value waypoints for alignment as well. Any shift in market milestones and course will have an impact on your value evolution as well.

I usually create waypoints for both current targets and suspect markets. We are focusing on our current targets, but it's good to check in with those suspects every once in awhile just to see if they've shifted in a more favorable course for us. That way we don't miss an opportunity. I use both tangible and intangible waypoints as markers, blending these aspects to get a true picture of market dynamics.

Tangible markers include all the usual milestones you'd review in selecting your market targets. These waypoint markers reflect the assumptions you made in your plan regarding each of your market targets and your suspect segments. Measurements include growth of the overall market and your available market (and the ratio between the two), your market penetration rates and growing (or decreasing) market share.

Intangible markers include the soft results you're seeing in your market. In creating your plan, you made some assumptions about how customers, competitors and others would react to your value and offering. Check those assumptions through a series of quantitative waypoints. If there's a delta, dive deeper to understand why the shift happened and its impact on your course. Markets shift for such qualitative reasons as confusion, changes in their own business course, or competitive actions, among others. Markets also shift due to sudden updrafts (that new product takes off and buying accelerates) or downdrafts (there are product problems; buyers are grounded due to the economy or regulation).

Waypoints allow us to monitor our success in small, incremental steps. They give us more control over our business, offering the ability to change sooner rather than later in smaller and more palatable ways.

When you find discrepancies in your waypoints, it's time to adjust your plan. That's the time to use trim tabs to realign for success.

Trim Tabs—The Stabilizers of Business Flight

The combination of waypoints and trim tabs empowers us to adjust our business course in real-time based on the dynamics in our markets. Like waypoints, trim tabs vary from business to business based on the specifics of the situation. Trim tabs come in a variety of forms; all are focused on small, incremental changes in a continuous fashion versus waiting for the next Big Bang adjustment.

For example, if we miss our product value waypoint for a new capability that's required in a market route, trim tab options would include:

- Assign extra resources to speed that value on its way. This means we have to realign the activity those resources were previously assigned to. But it beats the usual option of hoping we'll catch up and then falling farther behind. If this waypoint is critical to multiple target markets on our routes it's better to resolve the issue with small changes in resources than waiting until we need to take a more significant action.

- Replan for the next waypoint, shifting that requirement to a future delivery. If it's not a critical capability or it's in a noncritical market, we can wait a bit and see how things flow. We simply need to set our waypoints so that we watch that delivery carefully for any further slips.

- Hire more resources to get us back on track. If we don't have any spare resources and this is a critical value for our success, we must find a way to solve the delay or we risk our plan. That may mean shifting budget earlier into our plan or taking budget from another, less critical project for the short term.

Creating Your Trim Tabs

Trim tabs are defined in a dynamic way based on your progress against your waypoints. When you see a fluctuation—either positive or negative—in your progress against your plan, it's time to review trim tab options. When we review changes in our markets and our progress as we move through our flight, we become more dynamic in our forward progress, creating additional momentum, or gathering lost momentum, based on what's happening in real-time within our business world.

On the following pages, you'll find a few examples of waypoints and trim tabs applied to organizational, value and market measurements. These examples in no way cover all of the potential waypoints and trim tabs you will use. They are samples to help you think situationally about how to monitor and adjust your flight plan—as you fly. In each example, you'll see a sample waypoint, followed by two distinct trim tab options: one for reaching the waypoint ahead of schedule, and one for reaching the waypoint behind schedule.

Organizational trim tabs come into play whenever you miss a waypoint or accelerate a waypoint that is focused on your employees or the skills required to capture growth. We often overlook these waypoints and trim tabs, yet they are one of the fundamental requirements for sustained growth.

Trim Tab Option: Ahead of Schedule	Trim Tab Option: Behind Schedule
Waypoint #1: Hire required talent within one month.	
Examine how you can shift your plan to speed up results. Options might include product waypoints that were depending on hiring that skill set; increasing your financial waypoints thanks to a faster time-to-market; or expanding your plan to evolve at a faster rate.	You need to make that hiring happen quickly. Some options include dedicating a resource to interviewing and hiring; checking for underlying gravity in the hiring manager who really wants to keep his team as is; or adding resources and impetus (like a bonus) to get the hires completed.
Waypoint #2: All employees on board with new strategy within two months.	
You can most likely accelerate your plan, especially if your assumptions were heavily based on folks taking a long time to align with the new course. Look for trim tab changes that can speed your flight toward success in one or all of your market routes.	Trim tabs empower you to respond now versus allowing the issue to grow and cause major gravity. Options include face-to-face discussions with those who are still resisting the plan or potentially removing some of the naysayers before they destabilize your business.

Value trim tabs allow you to make small changes in your company, product and market values based on both your progress and your market's evolution.

Trim Tab Option: Ahead of Schedule	Trim Tab Option: Behind Schedule
Company value waypoint: Top 50% of profitable customers believe we have turned the corner and are a viable business within three months of relaunch.	
When you beat this waypoint, it's a sure sign you're on the right track. Leverage your customer support to accelerate your flight—you have market power behind you. Options include moving more quickly to address prospects that parallel these customers and leveraging these customers to turn around the curmudgeons in the market who still don't believe. Celebrate your success visibly and loudly. Customer support is the best proof of a turnaround success!	If you missed this waypoint your turnaround is at risk. The only way to turn around a business in the same, or similar, markets is with customer support. Options include assigning a SWAT team to go work with these customers and get them on board or assigning executives to specific customers to bring them back into the fold. Both options include asking these customers why they still don't believe—and fixing the issue.
Product value waypoint: Customers are buying a specific bundle as their first purchase, followed by options over time.	
They're buying even more and faster than we ever expected. It's time to take advantage of that behavior to speed up your plan. You can enter that next flight route earlier than expected or leverage those early profits to accelerate another focus area. Take advantage of the good news and don't just keep following the same plan. You have an opportunity to hasten your growth!	Customers aren't following the buying path you defined. They're slower and buy less than expected. Chat with customers and then decide what action to take. Options include repackaging your products to match their buying patterns; changing your forecast model to reflect a market slowdown for your revenue planning; or adding that one new capability they all want sooner to increase market demand.

Trim Tab Option: Ahead of Schedule	Trim Tab Option: Behind Schedule
Market value waypoint: Partner XYZ is in place and we're beginning to open that new packaged SMB market together.	
We're already selling together and the customers love our products and partnership. This is great news. It's time to accelerate things: maybe move on to the next route or expand your partnership to include another new market you planned to attack later in your flight. Leverage the opportunity that you've created through this positive waypoint.	We haven't been able to get partner XYZ interested. This is a BIG oops. If you were supposed to have that partner in place and running—and you aren't even in the door—your waypoint was misaligned in timing. You need to know that sooner rather than later. Options include targeting a different partner where you have a better chance of success, quickly finding leverage to get to partner XYZ or replanning your approach to that new market that required a partnership.

One point to note here: I don't always use company value waypoints. After all, our company value is our core focus; we don't change it that often. I do use company value waypoints, however, when I'm moving into new markets or to monitor segment value in specific segments of my market. I also use them for turnaround scenarios, as in the example above.

Market opportunity trim tabs help us make adjustments in our course as our target markets spin in new directions, our suspect markets come into alignment with our course, or new markets spin onto our horizon.

Trim Tab Option: Ahead of Schedule	Trim Tab Option: Behind Schedule
Route waypoints: Let's look at route #1 for BizTech as our example. For this route we had a waypoint of adding ten new SMB customers per quarter.	
We were adding 20+ customers per quarter. More than half of them were larger SMBs interested in the newer SMB product (bells and whistles from the new product, based on the older system). We added resources and moved forward in larger SMBs as leverage into small enterprise, since 25% of the new larger SMB accounts brought perfect market support for that effort.	If we hadn't been meeting those numbers, we would have (a) reevaluated our approach to find what value we were missing; (b) realigned resources to deliver that value; and (c) looked to see if we needed to reprioritize our focus, moving resources to a more profitable and successful route.
Route waypoints: Now let's look at the new SMB web and services market opportunity route.	
The web and services vendors loved our offering. Our twenty early targets couldn't move to the product fast enough. Within nine months we were the de facto standard for any SMB focused on delivering services over the web. We increased our investment and focus in this space and moved to capture a major new market opportunity—and high margin revenue.	Our product wasn't the fit we'd expected for the web and services business. There were some changes that needed to be made if we were to be successful. Luckily the changes were within our budget. We changed our plan, redefined the product, tested again and then moved forward. The same added value was applicable to the smaller SMB targets, leveraging our investment.

Emerging market waypoints are a bit different from other market oppor-tunity waypoints. These waypoints define what you need to see in an emerging opportunity market to make it viable. It's not always about your efforts; it may be about the market and its movement.

Trim Tab Option: Ahead of Schedule	Trim Tab Option: Behind Schedule
Emerging market waypoint #1: 10 large SMBs in place and successfully implemented; 1 enterprise partner trained and supporting our efforts.	
We had the reference accounts we needed and the expertise in half the time we expected. That meant we could accelerate our small enterprise efforts. Because we had created a separate team to focus on the enterprise we could move forward quickly into that space, enhancing our time frame without heavily impacting the rest of the organization.	If we had been slower in develop-ing the foundation we needed for the enterprise, we would have waited until after we had the right number of successful test flights and enough expertise to enter that space. If we didn't gather that foun-dation in a reasonable time frame, we would have rethought the small enterprise as an emerging opportu-nity and most likely refocused our efforts on another market.
Emerging market waypoint #2: Minimum of 25 small enterprise accounts in target industries proactively begin to engage with BizTech based on large SMB customer successes.	
Key small enterprises took note of our engaged large SMB custom-ers. We had 25 active prospects within three months of the launch of the new product and strategy. Now we could decide to enter the small enterprise full speed, focus on these 25 and garner success or wait a bit longer. We chose to focus on the 25—gathering market experience, credibility and valuable references.	Enterprise accounts just weren't interested in adding a new vendor to their already overloaded IT sup-port requirements. That meant we did nothing—and continued to watch the market. There's no rea-son to invest resources in a market that isn't ready for your company or your products when you have another significant market oppor-tunity to focus upon.

For example, with BizTech the small enterprise was really an emerging opportunity for them. They weren't ready for the enterprise at the time we were defining the strategy. So, we put together some measurements that would tell us when the market and BizTech's efforts were better aligned. These waypoints defined what we needed to have in place from our large SMB and small enterprise test flights to support our successful small enterprise mainstream market entry. It also defined what the market needed to do.

Waypoints are valuable only when they are measured based on real results and when we respond based on the truth of our situation. Don't continue on the wrong path because of excuses for your performance or the markets' performance against those waypoints. That just perpetuates a problem and lets status quo take over as your guide. Create a plan and waypoints that are reasonable and measurable. Then pay attention to that plan.

The goal is not to continue on our course no matter what happens. The goal is to find the most profitable course in the most effective way. Don't hang onto bad strategies; that only makes things worse. Even the best strategy can fail when the market changes drastically. If we're missing waypoints, or finding different market dynamics than we expected, something has changed within our organization or our markets. Don't fall in love with a strategy—evolve it! If you hang on for too long waiting for a recovery, that mistaken strategy becomes a vortex that sucks you down.

Evolve to thrive.

PILOT HANDBOOK: EVOLVING FOR SUSTAINABLE
GROWTH

1. **We must evolve how we execute our go-to-market plans.** Change in the
   form of Big Bang revolution can be replaced by change in the form of continuous evolution.

2. **First, bring your teams into alignment with your plan.** How?

   - **Share your vision.** Then focus on retraining the way your teams think
     about and execute change.

   - **Watch for gravity** in the form of naysayers—and eliminate it.

   - **Hire the expertise** you need to be successful.

3. **Second, proactively and continuously monitor your course.**

   - **Waypoints are real-world**, achievable measurements of small incremen-
     tal progress toward your destination.

   - **Waypoints act as your milestones of successful progress.** Waypoints
     show that your target markets are still in alignment with your trajectory,
     that your value evolution is in lockstep with your targets. They also act as
     opportunities to check on your suspect markets' courses, monitoring for
     closer alignment with your current trajectory.

   - **The right set of waypoints** assures the successful execution of your over-
     all plan. The wrong set can give you a false sense of security or a mis-
     guided belief that you're on track when you aren't.

4. **When a market doesn't respond as you assumed or you miss waypoints,
   you have a shift.** Don't keep following the plan that has you heading for a
   downdraft!

   - **That's when trim tabs come into play.** Trim tabs empower you to dynami-
     cally adjust your business course with small, incremental changes based
     on real-time changes in your markets and your own forward progress.

   - **Trim tabs are small adjustments that empower you to respond with min-
     imal disruption to your flight.** Trim tabs help you avoid the disruptions
     that come with Big Bang changes.

- **Trim tabs are defined in a dynamic way based on progress against way-points.** When you see a fluctuation—positive or negative—in progress against waypoints, it's time to review trim tab options.

The Bottom Line. Your goal is to find the most profitable course in the most effective way, not to stay on your current course no matter what happens. Pay attention to waypoints and enact trim tab options when you see minor fluctuations. Continuous change acts as fuel when flying toward sustainable growth.

CHAPTER 15

The Art of Strategy

The best strategy depends on the situation.

I wish I could give you a set of rules for creating sustainable growth. But there aren't any givens when it comes to defining great strategies. What works for one company may not work for another—even in the same marketplace. What works depends on the situation in your markets, the dynamics that evolve that situation, the specifics of your product and company value and the power you wield in a market. Those varied aspects create diverse potential combinations for your strategic actions.

The art of strategy helps you select the best routes from all of these potential combinations—creating your optimum growth plan. I find that the art of strategy is best learned through exposure and experience.

To that end, I've included a number of case studies in this chapter to reflect a variety of situations that occur in many businesses. We'll work through each situation, discuss the strategic options and pick the best growth strategy for each scenario. Each example is different, so you'll experience a broad exposure to strategic situational thinking in a variety of contexts.

Continuous Evolution Powers Sustainable Growth

Great companies realign continuously, leveraging their value in new and growth-oriented markets while also evolving to meet their current market's needs.

Let's look at the growth strategies of some recognized companies. This information is based on what we can see and read in the market. Then we'll focus on a couple of my clients where I have somewhat deeper and more personal insights.

 ## Dyson Vacuums—Finding Growth in a Highly Competitive Market

Dyson has long been known as the premier manufacturer of vacuum cleaners. Walk into any appliance store and you'll see the Dyson product proudly displayed as the ultimate cleaning experience. Their patented Cyclone technologies keep homes cleaner for those suffering from pet or dust allergies, as well as for the rest of us who just want clean. Within two years of releasing its first vacuum cleaner, Dyson outsold every other vendor in the UK. They just kept growing from there. Word-of-mouth marketing for Dyson is top-notch: every owner loves them, and every owner swears to all her friends that they should buy one too.

Vacuum cleaners represent a pretty tough marketplace for value pricing. After all, one's almost as good as another, and who wants to spend hard-earned dollars on something that hides in a closet 99 percent of the time! Dyson's machines were priced as the Ferrari of vacuum cleaners, with a target market focused on premier buyers who would spend big bucks. The company grew, but there was a larger market to capture.

With brands such as Hoover for the general public and Oreck entering the consumer space, it was pretty crowded and difficult to differentiate options. Everyone has the new HEPA filters and better motors for easier use; they've added the extensions for stairs and furniture; and they're mostly priced in the same ranges—and below Dyson's prices for their top-end line.

Yet Dyson continues to thrive. You can find their machines in forty-five countries. Their growth is no longer limited to their premier client spaces. They expanded their focus to attract other consumers, directly competing with the lower-cost vendors. And they are winning. How has Dyson lever-aged their core and segment values to create product value that's attractive to a broader range of consumers?

- Dyson's brand reputation is linked to their patented technology for cleaning. That same patented technology is available in every single vacuum they sell—from the most expensive full-featured machine to the slim-line version. Anyone who buys a Dyson knows they get that extra-clean value. That's a smart use of core product value across all markets.

- Dyson expanded their target opportunity focus; they still serve their premier clients, but they also offer something for everyone. They cre-ated a variety of machines designed to meet the needs and budgets of specific audiences, so a buyer doesn't have to pay for every little capabil-ity when they don't need them. There are vacuum cleaners for those of us dealing with pet hair, for carpet only, for a variety of floor surfaces and for stairs and furniture only. They can be canisters, uprights and even handhelds for the car or hard-to-reach areas. Dyson value is now packaged for a broader range of consumers and priced accordingly.

- Then there's the other innovation: the Dyson Ball. Every time I see the ad on television, I grin. It's a fabulous example of evolving product value by simply changing the package. But the Ball offers distinction too. Dyson recognized that a lot of us have tight corners and furniture that blocks our cleaning process. Nothing hurts my shoulder like running the vacuum cleaner into my piano leg. The leg doesn't like it either. The Ball eliminates those issues. Same powerful Dyson Cyclone technology, different package. But it's so much more than a simple package. It's a new way to clean, a distinction everyone sees the minute they walk into the appliance store. That bright yellow or purple Ball screams lighter and easier to use. Just look at it! Better yet, the entry-level machine is priced comparably to other mid-line vacuum cleaners. If you want more bells and whistles there's a Ball version for that too.

Dyson didn't dilute the premier price associated with their core value so that they could capture a larger marketplace. They packaged core value in smaller increments that matches the needs of specific buyers, then priced those packages to be affordable for each buyer segment. They broke down their total value into discrete packages of segment value for a suite of unique markets. They also added segment value that was compelling for many of us: the ability to move that Ball around any and every corner of our homes without the bumps and scars we expect. Now that's value evolution for profitable growth!

Fruit of the Loom—A Different Kind of Leverage

Fruit of the Loom is one of my favorite companies as I write this book. They are executing a breakout growth strategy as they come out of bankruptcy after being acquired by Berkshire Hathaway. They are aggressively evolving from their traditional focus on white boxers and briefs for the all-American male. Today, Fruit of the Loom is expanding its focus to a variety of market segments, leveraging enormous market creation dollars from a leading competitor to grow in newly emerging, yet complementary, markets.

Fruit of the Loom is a known and trusted vendor of men's underwear. Their product value rests in the comfort, durability and reasonable price. Their market value came from American males who wear their boxers and briefs and are proud of it.

But the underwear market has changed dramatically in the past few years. White boxers and briefs gave way to colorful patterns, silks and more. Men suddenly wanted a bit more color and excitement in their underwear. Designers entered the space with briefs by Ralph Lauren and bearing the polo logo. Suddenly, underwear was a status symbol! While the men's market was changing, the women's space watched as Victoria's Secret single-handedly created a mega-market for women's sexy underwear and lingerie, with a bit of comfort thrown in as well.

Fruit of the Loom's past had little to do with their future. Sure, some guys stuck with the plain white briefs, but many moved on to express themselves with fun and provocative colors and patterns. Fruit of the Loom had to evolve or ride their past all the way to the ground.

Fruit of the Loom hit the wall prior to its acquisition by Berkshire Hathaway. But now it's evolving in leaps and bounds. Fruit of the Loom expanded their value and focused on market segments that were underserved. The new underwear markets were created by the sponsors of those Vicky's Secret and Ralph Lauren models. Let's face it: none of us really looks good in what those models wear. Fruit of the Loom noticed that—and is leveraging it for growth in an in-your-face kind of way. Let's look at Fruit of the Loom's growth strategy.

- They followed the market for men's underwear, adding colors and new styles. They also kept the old standbys to maintain their customer base that just didn't want the frills.

- They broke into new markets. They targeted the female underwear market that Vicky's Secret had spent millions creating. Their distinction? Comfortable, soft, colorful underwear for those of us who don't have the Vicky's Secret body or who don't want to spend a fortune to have VS logos on our bodies. They leveraged the market creation power of Victoria's Secret to serve a large segment that viewed the brand as expensive and uncomfortable. Plus, gals buying their guy's underwear could now pick up comfortable, durable undergarments with more style and color.

- Fruit of the Loom created a series of advertising campaigns that brought the Fruits to life. Suddenly, the Fruits were, well, real guys who appealed to men, women and children. They were hip and modern—a stark contrast to the pure white, traditional look associated with Fruit of the Loom. My favorite ad these days is the Fruits reenacting Cirque du Soleil. We're inspired to see the Fruits singing as women of all sizes and shapes fly through the air in comfortable, colorful stretch cotton. I wouldn't try those moves in Vicky's Secret lace, but I would in my Fruits.

- That wasn't all. Fruit of the Loom further segmented the women's market by targeting the full-figured gals and offering soft, comfortable underwear designed specifically for their size needs. That's a market that Playtex has owned for decades and one that Victoria's Secret hasn't yet touched. With Fruit of the Loom, full-figured ladies can have the support they need while enjoying pretty, colorful and comfortable underwear from Fruit of the Loom.

- They also went after the kids' market, offering colorful prints and solids for boys and girls with their favorite characters and themes. As long as we're selling to Mom and Dad, why not bring the kids along as well?

Fruit of the Loom evolved by addressing complementary markets that were natural fits for a minor update in their product lines. That's a pretty savvy expansion strategy. They didn't really change their products; they added color and prints and new styles for women and girls, but that's not a huge shift. They focused on their core product and company value—comfortable, durable, affordable underwear—to serve their current men's and boys' market while expanding to address new yet very complementary targets. Their core remained the same even as their product lines evolved.

What did change drastically was their perceived company value. The plain vanilla, no-frills company is now hip, modern and innovative. Better yet, they make us all laugh with the fun ways the Fruits sing and dance to promote their underwear.

Fruit of the Loom accomplished a tough thing: they evolved a company brand and changed the perception of a global marketplace, without dramatically changing their product lines. That's market strategy at its finest.

 ## Big Systems—Growth in Search of Profits

Let's take a deeper look at Big Systems, my start-around client from chapter 2. As you'll recall, they developed custom systems and networks for very large government and research-oriented clients. They specialized in creating systems for specific types of applications that required lots of processing power—like weather forecasting, war and defense simulations and nuclear stockpile management, to name a few. They'd leaped into market power in the prior four years, quickly being recognized as the up-and-comer in these specialized powerful computers. Their growth had been phenomenal: more than 100 percent per year and still growing. They had so many orders for their systems, they'd nearly doubled their facilities and staff in the previous year, and they were doubling again as I came to work with them on a strategic growth plan.

If they were growing so quickly, why did they need me? Well, there was one big problem. Even as their revenues grew, their margins were declining faster than their revenues were growing. Indeed, they were coming close to losing money on every new contract they took. That's obviously not sustainable, so the company's CEO and board of directors asked me to take a look and make some recommendations.

The first thing we did was take a hard look at their value. We spoke with an optimum blend of customers, partners and internal folks who had their fingers on the market's pulse. We learned the following about their value:

Company: They were recognized as the vendor who knew it all about these sophisticated types of computers and applications.

Product: Their systems were trusted to show up and work—going into production weeks to months ahead of any competitive offering.

Market: They had very vocal customers shouting their praises, which is why they were growing so quickly.

What great value! Why the problem? We learned a lot as we chatted further with their customers and the client team.

- These systems were important to these remaining customers, yet as government entities, these customers always had to buy on a competitive RFP basis; the contract went to the lowest bidder who could supply the required capability.

- My client had a huge RFP response team who always knew just where to price the proposal to come in as the lowest cost vendor. That's right. They didn't price based on a required margin to the company; they priced to win the bid at the lowest price whether they made money or not.

- The sales team was focused on selling the next new thing, which meant that if the new thing hadn't been done before, they'd sell it just so the company could be the first ever to make this new approach work. That meant a constant investment in testing and finishing new technologies that weren't necessarily ready for prime time. That resulted in big overhead dollars—further reducing any opportunity for profit.

The company's status quo belief in growth first, profit later resulted in some pretty interesting business decisions. Most of the bids were at a loss, although no one wanted to admit that. Management explained it this way: "If we just keep growing, sooner or later the profits will come." That's not true in any business, especially when every product sold is priced below cost. We can never create enough volume to make up for that problem.

We also learned another shocker. Those government customers didn't care if my client made money or stayed in business. They simply wanted the lowest-priced solutions. Surprise, surprise. If vendors had to build those systems at a loss, that didn't bother these customers. My client was giving them what they wanted, and they loved Big Systems. But if my client raised their prices, they'd move on to another vendor without a thought. So much for customer loyalty.

A few things were pretty obvious by this point.

- Staying in the current market was not a profitable growth strategy. In fact, the more deals we sold, the more money we lost.
- Based on its current resources and staffing, Big Systems had to deliver far more margin to reach a break-even state—much less profitability.
- The company needed a new way to think about value and growth. Bidding on cool, never-done-before projects—at a loss—was not a sustainable strategy.

We had to find new market lift or we were going to be stuck riding a permanent downdraft. We spent some time releasing gravity and status quo and then took a look through fresh eyes—and we found those opportunities. Select commercial industries required the specialized power of these systems for collaborative design, review and analysis in manufacturing, as well as for production management in oil and gas—just to name two examples.

Commercial markets represented complementary segments that Big Systems could address with their current value. We did need to add market expertise in those specific segments and repackage our value in a few ways. But repackaging our value also helped us in our traditional customer markets. It forced the company to standardize its systems, providing more repetitive components and lowering overall cost on every system delivered to those traditional customers.

So what did we do?

Commercial Spaces: We defined a flight route into the top commercial segments based on aligning current value with market requirements and the segment's availability to Big Systems. These segments included automotive and aerospace, electronics and complex consumer goods manufacturing.

- We worked with experts and customers in the specific market segments to create the best short- and longer-term plan for our value.

- Since these were new markets for the company, we planned a series of test flights, first to gather experience and credibility, then expanding to target the mainstream opportunities for each segment.

- We hired experienced executives and staff in the commercial spaces to guide our efforts.

- We created a value plan for each segment route and began packaging systems to meet each market's specific requirements.

- We hired specialized sales reps to focus on specific companies as early targets in each segment, powering our test flights to gather experience, implementation expertise and market value in the form of customer references and credibility.

- As we achieved success in our test flights (based on our waypoints), we expanded to mainstream customer targets along those routes.

Within six months, we were successfully selling profitable systems into the test flight targets. Within a year we were selling into mainstream targets in all commercial segments, maintaining a 35-plus percent margin on every system sold.

Traditional Customers: We didn't want to walk away from our customers in government and research; we just needed a better way to do business with them. We needed to change the way we viewed their business while we changed the way they thought about us, as the vendor with the lowest price.

- We stopped the practice of bidding on every proposal based on the lowest price. We started bidding based on our cost—with a reasonable margin added. That was a big change for the team, but it was necessary for profitable growth.
- We let our customers know that we valued their business but that we needed to be profitable to remain a viable supplier for their computing needs. We explained that we would no longer lowball the prices for our superior systems.
- We worked with key customers to create prepackaged systems that they could order to meet their ongoing requirements, rather than defining a new configuration for every system they required. We worked with them to add their own specific software and other requirements to our systems. That move added value to Big System's computers by reducing customer efforts to install and test their own standard software.
- Big Systems continued to win the right deals, making at least 25 percent on each system sold to legacy customers. Big Systems also created distinct value through services, using their expertise to customize systems for unique applications. Competitors offered such services for a large price tag, but thanks to our experience we could do it for almost no cost, and it added high value.

We changed the flight plan significantly for current and new complementary markets. We may have sold fewer systems, but each was profitable. And the commercial sector was growing quickly, filling the revenue gaps (from the unprofitable business we stopped taking) with profitable, sustainable growth. We balanced the change in course, which is never easy to do. But sometimes you have to take a turn to sustain growth—or to stay alive. The key when taking that turn is to do it in a nondisruptive way, easing into it instead of making that abrupt Big Bang change.

Reviving a Market Leader—Back to Our Future

I mentioned earlier in the book that sometimes you do have to go back to 20/20 markets to go forward. I know that's a contradiction, but sometimes going backward is the only course available. Here's a case in point.

Take my client that was sliding downhill fast. Before I met them they'd gone from over $2 billion in sales to just shy of $500 million in a matter of four years. That's a pretty big downdraft. They were coming out of bankruptcy when I met them, led by a new CEO who had a whole different view of their marketplace.

Years ago they'd been a leader in the animation arena. But then new management came along, and they started focusing on the more mainstream systems, storage and networking markets that were "me-too," but that also represented the bright lights and big city to all computing vendors. We call them ego markets.

They'd shelved their technology—things that to this day make me shake my head and say, "Wow!" Thanks to their innovation, 3-D worlds could be created and shared across the globe by any number of users, all in real-time. Their software could change the world when it came to virtual worlds and entertainment.

So, what was the problem?

- As I said, they'd shelved all that high-value software. The most distinct value they possessed was sitting on a shelf, untouched for a decade yet still market leading. Now what does that tell you about the original decision to head for a commodity systems marketplace?

- They'd poured millions and millions into "me-too" system products that were selling at low margins. These products were failing to generate enough profit to keep the company in flight. And they kept pouring more money down that rat hole.

- They had one system product that was distinct—in a very small market niche. They were pouring millions into that product, even though it rarely sold at a sustainable profit level and it was focused on a very small market.

- The majority of the executive team was wed to the mainstream business. They didn't understand the power and potential of the animation and virtual world space. In fact, they believed it was a distraction away from their system focus. They'd actually convinced themselves they could grow the company with their "me-too" systems at low profit margins. Amazing what happens when status quo takes over, isn't it?

- They were still bleeding money, even as they cut staff and closed geographies to conserve and focus.

How's that for a challenge?

The new CEO understood the power of their intellectual property, and a couple of the executives saw the opportunity to pull this company out of the downdraft and back to a high-velocity flight. I was hired to help create the strategy and go-to-market plan to move this giant back into a leadership position.

What did we do?

- We created a route plan that focused on current customers and select partners for their initial return to animation. We needed credibility and a wow factor for the return flight. After we had our feet wet, we'd move into the broader and newer markets of virtual worlds, 3-D video events, entertainment and more—all with the help of those select partners and customers.

- We began to evolve the company value back to its roots—in animation. Customer audiences loved the solutions, even as internal players attempted to sidetrack our efforts. The status quo was strong here.

- We built a killer demonstration that was sure to wow every audience on a shoestring because there was little budget available. (The vast majority of the budget was still allocated to the low-profit and sliding-downhill systems business.)

- We showed our initial targets the products under nondisclosure and they went nuts. Everyone wanted some form of these products! In twenty years as a consultant, I'd never seen such a raving reception by customers and partners. What an opportunity!

- We launched to huge acclaim and had more than $60 million of quali-
  fied prospects in the pipeline within thirty days. How's that for a fast
  updraft?

- Everything looked great, but that all-powerful status quo was still working against this transition.

In the end, we failed. We did everything right in the market, but gravity
kept us down. Some of the employees remembered the good old animation
days. They were for the return to their past. But they were a big minority.
The majority of employees wanted to stay the current course. And so they
did. Management stayed the course as well. Everyone agreed with the new
course publicly and then diverse factions kept right on flying in their same
old direction. In the end, nobody won.

It was the strongest gravity I've ever experienced. This once-brilliant
company had the chance to shine even more brilliantly. Their value was distinct and market leading, in perfect sync with a huge and growing opportunity. Sustainable growth was right in their sights. But the power of the
status quo fueled the corporate infighting and sucked the momentum right
out of this soon-to-be-leader. It was sold for pennies on the dollar in one of
the saddest sell-offs ever in the technology industry.

BizTech—The Final Analysis

So what happened with BizTech? Well, there were ups and downs. The
attraction of the enterprise market was strong. Every other vendor was
playing there, and BizTech was continually distracted by those huge opportunities that promised fame and glory. It was a continual challenge to keep
everyone focused on the plan. But we did, despite a few stumbles along the
way. Eventually we had to release a few naysayers in management positions who refused to follow our new thinking, and thereafter, our forward
momentum and singular focus increased substantially.

BizTech grew in its SMB marketplace across all the markets we'd targeted. They strengthened their leadership position as they expanded their
product line to include everything from small, install-and-go systems for
SOHO audiences all the way to scalable systems for large SMB buyers.

Today, BizTech is releasing a next generation of products focused on the SOHO to SMB space. Their core value remains the same: a trusted expert for SMB business offering simple systems that just work.

They kept their focus, monitored their progress and evolved their course and value when the flight grew bumpy or when new opportunities shifted into their course. They soared despite the distractions because they focused and evolved.

In Closing

To defy gravity isn't as difficult as we assume it to be. When we release our status quo and think differently about our business, we continuously evolve to capture profitable growth.

You can soar to successful growth—*when you follow the principles of business flight.*

Release your sources of gravity, those status quo ways of thinking and doing that hold you back. Only by letting go of the myths and fallacies that pull us backward can we focus forward to capture new opportunities.

Find your fuel, your Value Mix that will drive sustainable growth. Don't rely on internal assessments. Gather input from the keepers of the truth—market and audience perception are the true measures of value.

Catch your lift, the market opportunities that are ready and waiting for your value. Define your Opportunity Horizon broadly, and then focus on the specific opportunity segments that represent your best chances for lift today—and tomorrow.

Plan your go-to-market routes, which will create the optimum leverage points for your flights. The more you can leverage your previous customer success, the stronger your power within any market segment.

Carefully monitor your flight, create and watch for waypoints that reflect your progress. Use trim tabs to make adjustments as needed to stay on the best possible course as your markets evolve.

Now evolve more. Nothing lasts forever—your markets, your value, your customer perceptions. Everything changes. So be prepared to continuously evolve if you want to reach for sustainable growth.

You can learn to soar the changeable winds that power your markets: ride the updrafts while you steer clear of the downers, leverage your lift and indeed, defy gravity.

SECTION II FLIGHT PLANNER

1: Create Your Value Mix

✓ **Question your current perspectives.** Begin by reviewing the above Pilot Handbooks concerning value and your Value Mix. Have each of your team members review them as well. Ask yourself and your team the questions about your value. Note your beliefs; we'll come back to them after we chat with your audiences.

✓ **Turn to the keepers of your truth.** Identify the audience members who will share their truths about your value—the good, the bad, and the ugly. Don't go to the same people you went to before. Get out and chat with new blood; that's where you'll find your opportunities. Be especially sure to ask a number of the uglies for feedback on what's missing in your value. Strong opponents can open your eyes to your best future opportunities—when you listen.

✓ Group your information gatherers into two-person teams (at a minimum) to gather input. From your keepers. Mix and match folks from different areas of your organization. Why? It's a great way to further reduce groupthink or gravity that may be developing as you move through the process. I often pair unlikely teams to shake loose the status quo. For example, team an engineer with a marketing leader and a sales rep to speak with emerging market customers and prospects. It's great training in the market, and you'll get a more balanced viewpoint.

I usually blend left-brain and right-brain thinkers in my teams. The best solutions usually come from a blend of both perspectives.

✓ Ask your keepers the questions found in chapter 10 and record each of their responses. Be careful not to let your own personal opinions enter into the discussions. Collect your keepers' feedback as it stands, no tweaking!

✓ **Draft a Value Mix.** Once you collect your keepers' perceptions, consolidate and analyze them. You'll see a pattern. And if you don't, then that tells you how confused your market is about your value. Take your keepers' perceptions and create a preliminary Value Mix based on their core and segment value inputs. You'll have more than 1 to 3 values, and that's okay for now.

✓ Now take a moment to compare audience perceptions to internal suppositions about your value. Pay attention to the deltas—the divergence between the two groups.

Don't look for agreement; that's the easy path. Look for the disagreements. Those areas usually represent pockets of gravity. Learn from them. Discuss how your perceptions differ from those of your keepers, and how to realign your own thinking to be more in line with your audience.

All too often we discount the input that is different from our own thinking. That's a sure way to send your business into a tailspin. Remember, audience feedback is what matters if you want to leverage real value to grow, listen and adapt.

✓ **Finalize your Value Mix.** If you find you have too many disparate, values it's time to have a serious discussion about narrowing your focus. Chances are that fragmented value is fragmenting your growth as well.

If you have different divisions with different value, create a Value Mix for each of them. Be sure to have a single company core value that every other division's value complements; otherwise, the fragmentation will work against you.

Creating your final Value Mix is one of the hardest assignments you can have. I often call these meetings "love-ins". The emotions can run high. Just remember, this isn't about supporting a belief that's creating gravity—it's about finding the Value Mix that will fuel your business's growth. Let go of those status quo beliefs and think objectively—and listen to your keepers.

✓ **Review your Value Mix with employees.** Dig deep to find disagreements and get them on the table. Unless everyone in your organization is behind that Value Mix, you're looking at an opportunity for big gravity. Even though you nipped a lot of that gravity as part of the section I exercises, use the Value Mix exercise to bring people even further into alignment with who you are as a business and how you will grow.

✓ Promote your Value Mix everywhere in your organization. Every employee should be capable of telling their family, friends, and anyone they meet about the value you deliver. One of my clients designated Value Cops to ask employees about the Value Mix in day-to-day operations. These cops recorded successes and failures on a Value Barometer. The cops gave away prizes for folks who were outstanding in their value statements. When the company reached a certain score, they held a big Value Mixer and everyone partied! Another client designed and printed posters of the Value Mix and displayed it in employee areas and in customer meeting areas. Their Value Mix became a focus of pride and communication among management, employees, customers and partners.

2. Identify Your Opportunity Horizon

✓ **Start by listing all of the markets you serve today.** Review each market segment and decide whether it's wishful thinking or a real opportunity. If you're not consistently selling at a profit to a market segment, be suspect of continuing to view that market as an ongoing target opportunity—unless it's an emerging market. Focus first on identifying your established *and* successful market segments.

Brainstorm with the best set of out-of-the-box thinkers you can assemble. Start in the abstract as much as you can and then work your way back to your knowns.

✓ While your teams are discussing value, also have them discuss opportunities for the future with your selected keepers of the truth. Don't limit their conversations with a list of leading questions. Get the keepers to tell you their story in free-flowing discussions, using the questions found in chapter 12. Too often we suggest what we want to be true in strict question-and-answer approaches. That's a sure way to limit the scope of feedback. Be sure to cover barriers to entry that the keepers see as issues. You can adapt to correct some issues and move on where there are insurmountable obstacles.

✓ **Assign a team to gather tangible data** on the market segments that are realistic short-, near-, and long-term opportunities. Use the questions for tangible inputs in chapter 12 to guide you. Be sure that the team includes a statistical analyst who understands how to create assumptions that reflect true market dynamics. Those assumptions are one of the most critical foundations of your plan; be sure an expert creates them. Use the results to size your opportunities and focus your priorities.

✓ Assemble all your feedback and analyze the results. Here's another tough discussion. Every business has markets that are its favorites—the knowns, the safe. But the safe markets aren't always your best opportunity for growth. Define your Opportunity Horizon with today and tomorrow as your focus. Then decide what markets from your past deserve attention moving into your future. Focus on growth opportunities. If you have a market that's waning—look at it as an opportunity for "cash cowing" as you evolve your business. You don't have to ditch your customers, just be realistic about what's profitable, what's growing and what's gravity.

✓ **Create your Opportunity Horizon.** Share that horizon with everyone in your company. That Opportunity Horizon represents all of your market potential—for the present and the future—based on today's situation. Show your employees how broad your opportunities can be and how limitless your potential can be. Put the focus on your priority markets, but also point out the abstract, emerging opportunities. It gets people thinking out of the status quo, creating a different focus for your future business. Just be sure you also explain how today's targets lead to tomorrow's growth (see question #4).

3. So how much can you really afford to do at once?

✓ This is one of the most critical steps you'll take. One of the biggest causes of downdrafts, tailspins and crashes in business is taking on too much. Don't do this. It's human nature to want to do everything quickly and easily. That nature gets in the way of viable strategic decisions.

✓ I usually appoint a couple of curmudgeons for this exercise. These folks are empowered to push and push and push again when applying resources to each segment's value bundles/requirements. Their job is to keep everyone in reality. Don't over- or underestimate; wishful thinking has no place in business planning.

✓ Take all of your projects and opportunities and plan them based on the examples in chapter 13. Be sure to plan for complete, compelling value advancements, not piecemeal tactical steps.

✓ Be sure to add padding for unexpected events. Get the curmudgeons to dig deep with the owners of the delivery resources. Look at past plans and note the discrepancies you've experienced. Allow for mistakes or slow deliveries—we all have issues that crop up. Rather than ignoring them, create a plan that can be successful even when the unexpected happens. If nothing untoward occurs—you'll be ahead of your plan!

✓ Leaders, it's really important that you let folks know that you want real-world estimates. Too many employees are trained to say they can do more than they can, realistically, in order to look good and to please their managers. Change this behavior if you want to succeed and grow.

✓ Double-check that you have every requirement planned for each segment you're targeting. I usually find someone who is working directly with that segment and who hasn't been involved in the specific planning and have them review the plan to make sure it's complete. You can't win if you don't have all your value in alignment and ready, so take extra care to be sure you have all your value bases covered.

4. What are your best routes for go-to-market leverage?

✓ The best strategy begins by identifying targets that are available to you and that bring immediate profitability. Look for those routes first. Likewise, look for new segments that align well with your value today. For new markets, be sure to create a route that includes a test flight to gather experience and credibility.

✓ Once you have your top priority targets, check for leverage across them. The more consistent your company and product values are across all your targets, the more leverage you have for growth. Also, the more your market value in one segment can compel a new segment to take you seriously, the better opportunity you have in that new segment. Note all of your leverage points and plot them for optimum effectiveness. I usually make a chart (based on the Opportunity Horizon charts in Section II) with points for each market opportunity placed in their relative positions: this is essentially the predecessor to a route map. Then I interconnect the points to show leverage among the markets. It may look like a spiderweb at first—that's good. Just adjust segment points until they show the best alignment possible: that's the beginning of your route map.

✓ Prioritize your routes based on reality. Overlay your value today on the routes. Too often we want to target a sexy segment, but we don't have all the required value in place to be a winner there. Double-check yourself to be sure you're being patient and practical. Avoid the bright-lights, big-city approach to prioritizing routes. Prioritize routes based on market opportunity and value availability—you can't have growth without both aspects being in sync. If there's a high-opportunity market but you won't have the value for months—plan an interim test flight. Don't fly full force before you're ready; you'll only crash and burn.

✓ Once you have your routes and their priorities defined, share them with everyone. Even if an employee never touches any customer, the more they understand about your flight and its routes and destinations, the more in sync they are—and the more aligned value and effort they will deliver. Post those routes (your immediate flight plans) right next to your Value Mix and your Opportunity Horizon. Help employees understand how your value applies to each route and how each route creates a foundation for moving forward on your Opportunity Horizon.

5. Am I on course? What am I going to do about it?

✓ So, you've created a tactical plan to execute the above strategy: assignments, timelines, measurements, and critical success factors. Now go deeper. We're all trained to set measurements and success factors that monitor the high-level, practical milestones for our forward progress. But if you look closely you'll find other, more detailed measurements that foretell our progress against those critical deadlines. Those are the waypoints we want to create.

✓ **Ask your teams to create their waypoints.** Take each critical milestone and add waypoints that offer early warning signals of success or problems. To ensure your success, train your teams to think about ways to evolve ahead of the critical point.

✓ **Brainstorm your trim tab options ahead of time.** Note that you'll need every trim tab you define at this point. The purpose is to teach folks to think about options for improvement on every leg of your journey. Once you have people thinking "what if" as they move forward, your organization becomes much more dynamic and prepared for incremental changes to assure success.

✓ **I usually create a war room for clients.** That's the place where we put our Value Mix, Opportunity Horizon, route maps, flight plans, waypoint measures, and any trim tab adjustments on the walls for anyone and everyone to see. I also use a very sophisticated method for tracking progress: red, orange, and green markers. Every week, team leaders (or their rotating designates) mark their forward progress. Green means on target; orange means trim tab options in the works; red means we're moving to a trim tab and everyone else needs to check on our changes to adjust their schedules. I also suggest that the team leaders (or designates) mark their progress together, discussing what's happening and what changes are required across the organization, and brainstorm with fellow team leaders concerning the best trim tab options for the situation. Formal project team meetings are one thing; this is a different focus. The goal here is to get the teams interacting and brainstorming change together. That process helps ingrain change as a fundamental part of your culture.

6. Expect change

✓ **Be prepared to evolve in sync with your markets.** How? Well, that depends on your situation. Some organizations need to reevaluate every month, some every quarter, some every week. The key is to have a process in place for reevaluating your overall forward progress, the relevance of your value, and the changes in your markets.

✓ Sometimes we create set teams to do periodic checks; sometimes we ask the entire employee base to make ongoing recommendations based on what they hear from customers, prospects, or others in the industry.

✓ **Train your teams to embrace change as part of their everyday environment.** Encourage them to constantly watch for ways to improve and evolve your value, market focus, and execution plan. These cultural changes make it easier to evolve while in flight. Changing the way we think in our corporate cultures is a key step to incenting continuous evolution.

As an international consultant, Rebel has worked with over one hundred clients—from larger companies to smaller, more entrepreneurial concerns—in a variety of stages in both the B2B and B2C markets. Her expertise focuses in three areas:

- **Ramp-Up and Roar**—Rebel has helped dozens of start-up and pre-IPO international companies gain a foothold in the right markets – where they have the strongest opportunities for significant revenue and leadership. During this time, she has developed proprietary, customizable start-up and launch systems to gain immediate market share in a variety of industries.

- **Rescue and Restore**—Because of her proven ability to rapidly identify and improve areas of high leverage potential, Rebel is the expert of choice for many venture capital and investment firms seeking turnaround solutions for their new acquisitions.

- **Redefine and Rejuvenate**—Rebel has spent half of her career specializing in "start-around" companies with great value—companies that needed to reinvent themselves to get past their status quo to grow in a rapidly changing environment.

Armed with diverse experiences and skill sets, Rebel Brown is uniquely qualified to quickly and accurately assess needs in a broad range of business types and situations to provide dynamic, effective solutions for high-velocity growth.

When she's not busy powering up corporate growth, Rebel enjoys her pursuits as an avid horsewoman, expert skier and outdoorswoman who tends an orchid greenhouse, hikes coastal mountains and kayaks the Pacific Ocean.

Visit www.RebelBrown.com to receive Rebel's weekly digest of thought-provoking and informative videos and articles.